P9-APA-734

by David Greenhood

« »

*Poems, et cetera*

*The Hill*

*Love in Dishevelment*

*Chronology of Books & Printing*
*(with Helen Gentry)*

*the Writer on his own*

# the Writer on his own

*by*
*david*
*greenhood*

University of New Mexico Press. Albuquerque

*Library of Congress Catalog Card No. 72-80754*

*First Edition*

*to Evelyn Harter*

# Contents

## *Foreword*

THESE IDEAS ARE OFFERED *for the working writer rather than for literary students whose main concern is, usually, learning how to judge other performances than their own.*

*The "you" is in most instances myself. But many of the thoughts were occasioned by some other writer, often one seeking either a suggestion of what to do about an encountered difficulty or a confirmation of an intended departure. I soon found myself supposing that his case were mine and I would take to soliloquizing about it as a workaday matter.*

*Probably all speculative writers talk to themselves. When they are in the act of writing, though, they speak to themselves most significantly. For when a writer asks himself how he'd best express his meaning, he is asking not merely just what that means to him but what and how much he can mean to it. Toward that kind of significance my principal interest has tended.*

*The working writer is always at work. The more he trusts in the authority of his imagination the more he must devote himself to the mastery of his individual kinds of hardship. His exigent concern in every poem or story he writes is that of living through it—both the task and the result. The need to do so may be the chief reason why he would care to ponder any of these notes.*

*The arrangement of matters in a sequence of chapters should be regarded as a tentative accommodation rather than a nicely schemed development. Each of the notes occurred to me by itself at one time or other, without program. I should like to share this experience with my reader, whom I invite to skip around as much as he pleases, mixing my thoughts with his own—taking plenty of credit for them. If he disagrees with me on any point, I hope that when he refutes it to his satisfaction he will gain some freshened perceptiveness which may not have come to him if we had not differed.*

# Tempt the devil

Because to be human is to be wayward, our life is more interesting than it might have continued to be in Eden. Man's irregular curiousness in that perfectly regulated park was his tumble from blissful status but also his outward move.

Once he had made that venturing break, he was on the move for all time. Throughout all creation.

« »

As in two-footed walking, every move of an imaginative mind begins with half a stumble. And we stumble oftener than when we walk.

« »

Only in the likelihood of error is there life. Here. Now. *Our* form of life.

« »

Doing something the wrong way just to see what may happen may kick out into view a hidden object. The way to become consummately stupid is to do (also to have) everything obediently right from our earliest years. Try for niceties last, if ever.

« »

Latency is an ever-teasing concern of a willingly realizing mind.

« »

A valiant writer lets his mind have its full span between sanity and madness.

He does not avoid extremes or try to keep the middle tack. He does not stay put at any safe place in his psychic range. He does not engage himself with avoidances.

*Tempt the devil*

« »

If we suppress our wackiness we'll seal off the source of some of our most truing impulses. Our potential will dwindle. We'll no longer feel the sweet daze and speed of the push of it.

Then in the misery of our loss of freedom we'll hate freeness. We'll move only in straight, strait lines, turning only at right angles or in rigidly measured departures from them. No use to tell ourselves then that we are conservative, for we save nothing; or that we believe in classicism, if we don't enliven its continuation. We'll be conceitedly atrophic.

« »

Gambling, simply because it is diverting, can have some salutary results. The best of these is that it can accustom us to the natural fact of losableness.

Every time we attempt to write in what is not a tedious repetition of a petrified mode, we gamble. We must learn to do our gambling gamely: with the intent to increase our hardihood when we lose our stake.

This hardihood gives a writer his nobility—in the full meaning of that word, back to its earliest.

« »

It does little good to be wholly certain before going ahead with writing, either a novel or only a paragraph.

Nobody can blueprint spontaneity. Without that, we work like copyists instead of like authors.

To begin by being mentally lithe is always better.

Adamant assuredness, not the topic, is what makes bores.

« »

Let us be willing to lose some reckless bets on our wise selves. A sure bet is no bet at all for the writer who wishes to get wise to his follies. And perhaps discover some wise uses for them.

Much of a writer's wisdom is what he has extracted from his foolishness.

« »

It is not always easy to distinguish between one's intuitions and one's fatuous notions. Or between an inner prompting and some obsessive arbitrariness. Or between having a way of one's own and having one's own perverse way.

At the outset, it is not always necessary to discern such differences. The inceptive necessity is to feel started and to take to the going. Even if that going is not an excitation but only an intensifying stillness—a deepening.

« »

Intellectual honesty is almost the rarest kind of honesty. The very rarest is the artist's. An all-out fiction writer must have both kinds.

There is also the need to look for and invite one's possible dishonesties. These often come in disguise. The ones to watch for most are really honest in essence but have the appearance of being the opposite. Besides, he must be able and willing to know how it feels to be dishonest in other ways than he himself has been. Unless he can imagine well the compulsions of wrongdoing he will be too slightly aware of too small a part of human existence to tell as great a story as is waiting for him to write.

## *Tempt the devil*

Every creative* writer must search out of himself further honesties and dishonesties than those which convention already has names for, if he wishes to be amply conscious of his forces. And to have more and more access to his reserves.

« »

An idea as it first occurs to us is likely to dissemble itself. Some of the knack in presenting a story is in how we humor and reverse these dissemblances.

« »

We must accept gladly the fact that the imagination is an exorbitant consciousness. We can begin to imagine only if we are ready to welcome excesses.

« »

A half-conscious hope with beginners is that somehow they will write better than they know. As one matures, one's consciousness of that hope increases. This happens because in maturity one's respect for one's potential deepens. A deepening respect for potentials is what happens as one's appreciation of poetry and fiction ripens. Likewise one's appreciation of oneself as a writer.

*This word has been used almost to death by commercial knaves and pretentious dunces. Here we must restore to it its whole meaning, which is our means of survival. And our means of grace. For a writer can be an atheist, and yet when he sets out on a creative, rather than a replicative, task he is as a poet or a novelist in a state of mind that is like that of prayer. Creation is precarious. In it we are asking and awaiting, and are at an extent of avid consciousness. The act of writing as we would write is in its inception a life-or-death move, a taking charge of growth. Under our hand there's a fresh growing, or there's nothing. Unless we believe this we can't learn about our art anything worth a tinker's curse.

« »

In writing poetry we keep approaching what we know we cannot know, but we keep on because we feel an inexplicable assurance that it is worth knowing. This anticipation of that worthiness is probably what functions within us as a remote mentor, imparting to us the skill which surprises us—and others.

In writing fiction this happens, too, but discreetly behind the story, clear away from the characters, not within it, as it may within a poem.

« »

It is easy for a reviewer to point out wherein a writer is wayward, too arbitrary, strikes poses, affects mannerisms. (It's even easier than being guilty.) But it's not easy to understand how a fault may originate in the productive plight of a writer whose task has dared him to exceed his comfortable habit. Exhibitionism is ordinarily a habit of making up for some concealed weakness, but in an extraordinary writer the outward fling of an ostentation can pull forth a hesitant vitality.

There are some moments when a writer must either take a chance of tending toward badness, so that he can regain the feel of his vigor, or else go from one flat rectitude to another.

« »

To be a writer worth more than mere luck, you have to expose yourself to luck. Tempt the Devil and expect angels.

One may no longer believe in muses or divine messages but unless one lets himself open to the possibility of forces other than those he knows already, his desire to exceed his ordinary self through extraordinary writing may be cheated.

« »

"Have I any talent, or haven't I?" That's not the question. No more than whether or not I/You should *be*. Such questions are the wrong ones to ask to do our questing for our latent fires.

Those queries are the kind that customers ask: "Should I buy it?"

(Should you buy yourself? Why not? You have to. But you don't have to sell yourself.)

The real question is, Am I willing? Or only willful? A willing writer is a ready writer. Ready even for tough luck.

« »

Our main effort should be to imagine forth, rather than to be always backtracking. Ruing. Picking up stuff that fell off because we were overloaded or so badly loaded that we couldn't carry it.

« »

In order to work a little easier we must play a little harder. For example, we need to play with words, often strenuously, recklessly. In ways that to anybody else would appear atrocious. This limbers and strengthens us to work with the no-nonsense words masterfully.

A going writer often has his private puns, some of them so outrageous that he'd like to clout an inquisitor with them. Yet they enable that writer to reach into extra directions. Though they're just a (private!) gimmick, they serve as a kind of secret cross-reference system within his head's chaotic vocabulary, such as would wreck the system in his favorite dictionary. But also such as improves its own system for him especially.

« »

Thoughts have tendrils. There's no certainty as to what they may cling to. And grow upon, perhaps parasitically. Or, reciprocally, grow with.

« »

Great thinkers, logical as they may try to appear in public to be, often do some aimless writing privately. It expedites their cogitations. An unheard of theory, say, occurs to mind and they play with it by "writing it out" merely to see where it will lead. It usually leads nowhere. But the chances are that, much later, a fine work will owe its success to this seemingly self-indulgent exertion.

Pestered by the memory of former sallies that came to nothing, we may forbid ourselves any more random writing because we think it's a pointless use of energy. But it isn't if it begins from actual impulse, which in itself is power, the kind we can keep only if we heed its presence. It's the unused impulses we really "lose," rather than the spent ones.

« »

Wayward tendencies are not invariably pernicious. Those more difficult to avoid than to permit, such as temptations to take side trips, can prove profitable. The very fact that they're *distractingly* interesting may make them exploratory. The hazards of digression then become an onward pull. (Hazards? Why not? If we want our mastery of writing to be a guided tour we don't want it to be truly ours.)

Sound literary discipline does not require that a writer go like a railway rather than like a nose-happy dog.

*Tempt the devil*

« »

The active mind of a writer is seldom without sidewise tugs from matters that are off the strict course of his theme. The reason he doesn't ignore them in his *thinking*, much as he may exclude them in his writing, is that he wishes to feel breadth within himself as he works. This is how what he does put down in perhaps simple, unramified writing can have strength and spread of connotation, intrinsic magnitude.

« »

To be in the habit of feeling that there are going to be some risks is a salutary uneasiness. The best performers confess they always feel their butterflies before going on stage. It's a sure sign to them that they still have within them the crucial concern it takes to do their job well. Each performance is one more chance to hit a supreme point.

« »

To feel the push of an impulse is in itself wonderful, and it is better yet when there's a sensing of possible danger in it.

The writing process has its own drama: it's a succession of anxieties.

The suspense as to whether your story will survive the vicissitudes of its production intensifies your interest in it, and this strengthens you for achieving the suspense that you wish to take hold of the reader. There are writers, otherwise proficient, whose fiction is weak because they can't bear the suspense, the agony of it, their characters would have to suffer; and this same softness keeps such writers from taking up the challenge of the kind of story that might force them to strive beyond mediocrity. For if you shun the crucial, you're afraid to do any very vital writing, be it fiction or poetry. Some of your best poems-to-be dare you to write them.

« »

We must have the nerve it takes to commit the Promethean crime, even though there is little likelihood that we shall ever have to. Every faculty a writer has within him waits for his courage.

« »

Sometimes upon emerging from inertia we suddenly realize that we already know more than we can be taught. Our imagination, we feel, must have leapt ahead and then our reason caught up with it. We made a break, and our skill coincided. This feels good.

# Being wayward without losing one's way

What is lacking in writers who have chosen to do only the conventional, sure-to-sell thing is courage. They may have talent, imagination, diligent training but will not venture into uncharted regions. It's a dread of getting lost. Or of facing again the unknown as they had to at their outset, thankfully now long past.

There's a kind of satisfaction in keeping alive through the sales of what one writes, and this helps to sustain also a productive morale, but to alter one's inner cast in fear of not succeeding in the market is to take so much caution that it becomes an imprudence.

The same is true of the fear of not responding to the dazzle of a profitable elite with its latest literary theory. Or of not kowtowing to the over-reassuring proprieties of "the Tradition" whenever it is once again awesomely displayed.

« »

The sanctifications of success have deluded many artists into feeling there's something disgraceful about a failure. And that *feeling* is the worst failure of all.

One must learn how to *honor* oneself through failures. Each defeat makes us that much more of a veteran if we brave it through. It gives a writer a secret dignity. There's no secret and no dignity a writer needs more.

« »

The false and the true occur together everywhere and in everybody. The two seem to imitate each other.

A trustworthy writer sees this as a fundamental circumstance in the human part of the universe.

All minds have to discriminate between the true and the false throughout the days and nights; it is not the duty of the artist particularly to do so. He must cope with both, which is why his life is not an easy one.

« »

We can take a mighty hint from the paths of apparently errant objects in the curvature of space. What appears off-path is still true to its way of existing in movement. There is no caprice here.

« »

In a poet an act of the imagination is an act of faith. If he loses this faith he too is lost.

« »

A writer must continually admonish himself: "Go back to childhood as much as you need but not to your days before toilet training. And don't leave your toys on the stairs."

« »

New knowledge entails expulsion from the estate of indolence. And out into the fields of hard work.

So much of the literary process is hard work, we speak of a writer's "works."

« »

Writing is the employment an able writer likes best because it's what he can do best, and do his best in because it's what he likes to work his hardest at.

He may not like drudgery but he's unashamed of its necessity for him. To be *willing* to drudge is part of his ability to write well.

« »

Writing better than you know! This is possible, no matter how much you know. Never does it depend upon how little.

No retreat from industry and intelligence will favor that miracle. Once you have written better than you had known you could, you are burdened for further task.

« »

To get started we must have utter release. An unfettered intuition is the only kind possible. But once it is "out," it becomes a control as we continue to work with it.

What began within our feeling of abandon can become an appreciable reality and continue so only as far as there is a steadying maintenance of vigor going on. This is quite different from willful constraint and the pedantry of externalities—to avoid which we don't have to go crazy.

We have to be alert. We are handling power.

« »

A writer is privy to his inner power. Nobody else can know the feel of it. Nobody else can know just how it demands to be handled. We must have no dread of being alone with it. Each of us must insist upon the recognition of this solitarity.

When we fail to manage our own power, there is but one fault that anybody else can point to as the probable cause. It is the consciousness, often only the suspicion, we may have of some important deficiency. Our affectations, mannerisms, posturings, deceits, and bullyings have their origin in that secret embarrassment.

« »

If a writer cannot repair a deficiency in himself, he is better off to own it. No use to hide it or disguise it. Or make a virtue or an aesthetic creed of it. What's the use of wrestling with an absent angel?

An inability to invent plots does not alone disqualify a writer. Nor does the inability to think up startling figures of speech. Or to come upon profundities. The lack of single gifts is not a disgrace—only the faking or flaunting of them is.

It's always better to be plain than to mangle one's style by forcing envied but uncongenial traits into it. For the absence of integrity can become boresome reading. One is less likely to be mediocre because he is unaware of lacks than because he is content with a mass of pilferage.

« »

In a creative person's rebellion the action is eruptive for change. As with the geologist speaking of "disturbance" as a factor in the forming of mountains, it has a positive aspect.

The mood is at first more for ridding than for smashing. A writer may say, "Not until I told myself to hell with all that stuff, did I find out what I could do." And he did. That is, unless he mistook the noise he made for the discovery of what he could produce. No matter what freedom a ridder may feel, it will produce nothing if he hasn't already had within him that which can be evident only in freedom.

« »

The presumption that one is a genius disables more writers than does the failure to discover one's genius.

# *Being wayward without losing one's way*

« »

An artist must summon his imagination, skill, and courage to exceed the norms and transcend the standard, but only his anger or bent for mischief to violate them.

« »

When we succeed in speaking without resort to affected mannerism it seems to have been the easiest ploy of all. This is because self-trust puts us into connection with our own best resources.

Affectation is self-evasiveness. It is being wayward from one's own identity—an almost meaningless phrase unless we think of having a kind of inner compass which, though it responds to outer forces, is itself a force.

« »

It isn't a matter of whether your critics and public will or will not ever detect your spurious excesses. (You may be sure these fatuous indulgences will themselves find you out sooner or later.) What matters is that they are dissipative instead of liberating. With them you get yourself into a state of jejunity, an emptiness that only a fervent writer can know the hell of. A wretchedness worse than that of blockage, in which you can feel that there's at least storage. But when you are emptied because you faked an excess, then what you had thought was a release from inhibition turns into a feeling that you had nothing to inhibit.

And probably you had plenty. What became of it? It was denied. For the sake of false show. Or even a meticulous adulation for an overbearing orthodoxy—which could as likely be dictatorial modishness as old school.

« »

As a modern writer matures he finds the age he lives in is ethically more wayward than himself. In anger he may decide to be more wayward than it at its worst. It has hurt him badly.

Perhaps he feels it has demoralized him to such an extent that, in desperation, he can do no other than spitefully retaliate with further demoralization: excrete his own nastiness and rub the world's nose in it.

(Perhaps he may do this merely to attract attention, pretending all this grievance and "alienation," as he sees many other misguided writers successfully doing, and then indeed he does succeed in becoming worse than the world.)

What then is achieved? Nothing. Nothing but tantrum. Well, there are readers who admire a magnificent tantrum, pay their money for it. And that's the whole payoff: cheat in exchange for cheat, dung for dung.

« »

Extraordinarily rich talent, keen intellect, quick skill, and early recognition are sometimes the luck of extremely disagreeable persons who may in no way except one deserve all this: they spare themselves no more than they do anybody else for the sake of their work.

Fortuity is unfair, else it wouldn't be fortuity. A thorough artist's devotion corrects that.

The time comes when most of us must accept the fact of a natural deficit in ourselves as writers. We recognize our fated shortcomings bitterly or bravely—or both. Perhaps we quit. Fortuity doesn't, though. There's no telling what may not still occur to us: what rarity. And what peculiar fitness we may chance to have for it. A writer's best self-favor is his willing readiness.

*Being wayward without losing one's way*

Appraise well your adversity-bred hardihood, for lack of which many a hitherto luckier hand has been stopped forever by one or two defeats.

« »

Among the finest writers, there are two main differences of feeling about the nature of their art. Some believe in the existence of absolutes. Others reject that belief as being a rigidifying mental habit. Accordingly, some like to have rules, others abominate the idea of recognizing any.

Whichever way a writer is disposed, he can either gain or lose by it. That depends upon whether he decides to be a willing artist or only a willful one. It's a choice between effort and indulgence, which of those he prefers as a private custom.

He can't, and shouldn't, expect of himself all of one always and none of the other ever. Yet he must keep reminding himself which shall be the dominant.

If he doesn't deeply desire mastery he is wasting what great or small vitality he may have. This respect for one's potential mastery is necessary even to the mystical writer who feels that he's "merely the instrument of a higher power."

« »

What really does a writer good is to watch a fine musician or dancer "practicing." This may seem an unappealing word for the steadily productive relationship going on in an artist between his thinking-self and his doing-self. Here, though, is more than dutiful "exercising"; here is also devotion. *That* counts.

Practice, discipline, diligence can't always be depended upon, it's true, to gather up our loose ends or to kick loose a block, for so much of what and how we write must still be left to luck. But we have this one certainty, and it's the other way around: *without* these observances we must expect grief.

« »

Whether to write a million-word epical novel rather than some short stories is not a question of courage. One can know one's own courage in a creative challenge only by how willing one is to endure humiliations in trying for envisioned but hardly reachable qualities.

One may need self-conceit to have self-confidence for the challenge. (This is why we should not deplore our own or any other artist's egotism.) Such faith is not vanity however sorely failure may make it seem to have been in vain.

The dire mistake is in gauging quality by size, greatness by bigness. The quality of our courage anticipates the quality of our performance; neither is the measure of the other. It takes fine courage to write a fine short poem rather than a monstrous long one; we may not feel our bravery in the first instance and feel nothing else in the other.

« »

No acquired knowledge is inhibitory if it has become one's own. Making it such restores its creative phase. And it is made one's own by one's creative forces.

Intuition works not out of ignorance but out of what one already knows.

Knowing is a process, a working. Unless one works with knowledge and keeps it working with one, there's really no having of it. It's energy, not stuff.

## *Being wayward without losing one's way*

« »

A developing writer must have ways of not skidding into utter wantonness.

He must be able to relax fully without slumping at all.

He must teach himself how to feel free without slipping headlong into his own torrents of arbitrariness.

He must not break out of confinements only to get lost in looseness.

He must value his compulsions but not let them shove him around for only their own sake.

Good production comes out of the assurance of discerning one's true urgencies, and out of *using* their force, instead of recklessly spending it.

« »

An abundance of talent can become a surfeit. The blessed stuff can be turned on too much at one time, like water pouring too fast so that when the cup is drawn away it holds less than it could contain.

« »

It's a dire pity to fail to develop from amazing exhibition into solid, lasting importance—that is, greatness. To just miss becoming great is a sorer grief than to fall short of ordinary success.

If the classical poet had any deeply felt intent in his private ideas as to how he should write, it was not control for the sake of control, or perfection for its own sake. It was that he should not waste in vulgar display the gifts that the gods had bestowed. For all their largesse, they were not extravagant; for all their pride, not vain. They were great and he was a mortal entrusted to exemplify such greatness. And it was only through unity, clarity, proportion, and immense care that he could manage to do so with the overload of riches they had put upon him.

« »

Many of us have a habit of interrupting ourselves in ways we would resent as bad manners if done to us by anyone else. But the rich, active mind feels again and again the press of matters from many sides. Suppress the urge to interrupt and you take the life out of conversation and writing.

The tendency to interpolate, to chink parenthetical matter into our text, we can indulge to our frustration but prohibit with much loss.

What, then, makes this essential mental eagerness bad? Compulsive total recall. Exhibitionism. Didactic jabbings. Misdirection. Disproportion. What makes it good? Accommodation. Spur. Relevant wit. Tone. Grace.

« »

Revery is an agreeable pastime a writer may enjoy by himself but had better not make a show of in public.

It's often a mockery of meditation and should not be mistaken for it or offered as such.

It is willful somnambulism. Instead of behaving in sleep as though we were awake, we behave like a sleeper while we are wide awake. It's a helpless floating downstream. Although it is offered as effortless enjoyment, it compels readers to share this helplessness. That's why it bores.

« »

Good artists love to be lazy once in a while, but their art doesn't. Laziness is an amenity only when it's smug. One of the delights of being an artist is that the exertions are the most opposite kind of amenity possible.

« »

If a self-training writer wants to give himself a hard workout to improve his skill he should try his hand at fantasy. Whether it be a fairy tale for children or a science fiction story for sophisticates, no other kind of prose permits so much waywardness of mind and yet requires so much control of hand.*

Writing fantasy—effective, durable fantasy—is not a trifler's pastime. It demands wiser indirection than mere vagrant loafing affords. It may by chance begin in one's head as revery but by the time it gets down on paper it becomes a rigorous exertion.

You have to be something of a realist, rather than an evader of reality, to write fantasy.

The mental doodling that may have occurred beforehand must positively shape up or be cleaned away.

A fantasy, if we hope to put it over, must have a logic of its own, even if it's only a quasi logic. This too takes some doing, a way of being wayward and still getting some place that's fine. A fantasied quasi logic cannot be the least bit sloppy.

Although for the nonce we may be heedless of time and space, of history and physics, we must have a sprightly cleverness that we manage with special care for consistency of artifice, such as a strengthening pattern, an onward rhythm, just as much congruency in presenting fancied facts as would be expected if they were actual facts.

*All types of fiction we can profitably regard as fantasy, at least from the writer's view but not necessarily as the reader later sees it.

The more extravagant the characters, the more controlled must be the plot. The more arbitrariness we depict, the less of it we claim.

« »

To be sportive in writing, we must be both delicate and strong, both free and precise.

« »

Many a supposedly serious writer has within him scarcely any earnestness except perhaps for grabbing attention and big pay. Many a grim story is nothing better than heavy whimsy. It parcels out chunks of realistic scene, speech, and event for any easily "disturbing" effect it can piously justify with the slogan that "the truth hurts." Any queer violence goes if there's some mumming about "The Existence of Evil." This is the same fake artistry used in the resort to patriotic and religious clichés for the opposite, "good," effect. Despite such ostentation to appear serious, the writing does not stem from earnestness; for all its "documented" accuracy it continues to be irresponsible fantasy.

Genuine earnestness stems back into the depths of a writer's main preoccupations. These usually have to do with being alive, mortally alive, and fallible.

All the preoccupations are felt more than understood, and although the main effort is to understand them, the writer must feel them in order to empower this effort.

They brew earnestness because he, being mortal but very alive for the present, knows that whatever he may utter, whether stern or gay, will be potentially his last words. So he maintains a most intensified sense of being.

*Being wayward without losing one's way*

« »

A writer's earnestness sooner or later overtakes his sallies of abandon. This happens because of his valor in facing the difficult. And because he knows he has this valor his abandon is the more joyous.

« »

A writer's expressiveness is largely the result of his having trained himself to tackle what seems too hard to say, the very things which those who have too much facility and too little earnestness dare not attempt.

Much facile writing that may over-impress you with its selling success is soon pushed away by more of the same, of which there's ever an oncoming supply.

Take a slow stroll through some secondhand bookshops or flea markets, and note well the dead books there. The more of any one of them you find, the better it sold in its little day.

« »

The parental botch, all-out permissiveness, should be a warning to us writers who are trying to bring ourselves up.

Total permissiveness in any art is as bad as total regulation.

Only if a would-be writer is vacuous and subconciously suspects that he has nothing to give will he neglect to realize that creative freedom is never careless. If he has plenty of talent, or only some that's minor but valid, he will sooner or later, despite mishaps, wish passionately to take hold and get on, desiring not only scope but to be his own man in his art. Both his instinct and his experience will convince him that out-and-out arbitrariness is abortive of art.

« »

We may wisely abominate overmuch whimsy but if we press too hard in forbidding ourself the fun of it, some of our liveliness may be the cost. There's a unique glee in letting go of everything rational, decent, and even sacred, for a single sparkling second, then recovering just as sprightlily. As a brief aberration, a whimsy may loosen a tightness from being too long on a strict line. It can even test the reality of that line. Children are always ready for a bit of it with which to test codes and ostensible verities, to see whether any such may not be whimsies too. Any whimsy, however, is only fun for the nonce. Momentariness is of its essence.

As a habitual indulgence whimsy is pernicious to the working-health of an otherwise very good writer. It tricks him more than it does his readers. If its quickness of effect tempts him into using it as an easy, oft-recurring device, it becomes a perpetual cheat. The whimsy addict seeks release from his aesthetic and rational responsibilities. That is why the genre has been denounced as "avoidance of life."

« »

However metaphysicists and psychologists may figure it out, we have within us what seems to many of us writers to be a vast chaos. Probably, whatever it is, it only seems to us chaotic, as the Galaxy seems, and like that, isn't. Anyhow, to think of it as an inner, or central, chaos is a good working notion of it.

Once we accept and respect our inner chaos, it becomes a source of vitality. We then feel we're full of something, something that must somehow be told, even if we can't at first determine exactly what it is. It is so mixed, so disordered that it engenders in us a yen for sorting and ordering. This is what we feel is "saying." Actually, we hanker to "*say*" before we want to "tell." This hankering to *say* is the poem inchoate, which always precedes the tale if a good story or finished poem it is going to be.

This phenomenon is not self-expression; the preoccupation here isn't with selfhood but with *form*. We are driven sane by this hunger for form—this Something Intact. Something brought outside ourself, something to be other than ourself. And somehow right in its own right.

« »

Writing is not the mummification of utterances. A writer who is really a writer doesn't use the page before him, or the book page he hopes it will become, as if it were a catch-all tape recorder. He respects the literariness of literature* because writing is itself a *form* of saying; a form in which at the very moment an utterance is set down, it is already memory and belongs to the mind, the mind with its holding and using function and not merely its catching function.

A writer in earnest knows that behind his every caprice is a desire that turns it into that kind of experimentation which is his craving for form. He can't be content until "it takes form"—until he has "got it into shape" so that he feels he "has hold of it" and has made it deliverable as an entity.

He may be iconoclastic, intent on decrying forms that have become irksome formulas and formalities, but that doesn't mean he is repudiating form. And he'll not feel he's doing a good job of demolition unless the way he does *this* achieves form. Its own.

« »

The complexity of our natures, the persistence of our animalhood,

*Including preliterary literature, such as the ancient poetic and prophetic works, which were learned by heart—that is, "written on the heart."

somehow constitute in us a wisdom that in the long run prevails over our freewheeling folly. If we care very much about being writers, the tendency toward the organic is stronger than any away from it. If we desire skill, its prime intent is toward composition.

Our very dream of achievement is an anticipation of form, and the more that dream takes form the more we want it to come true.

We are so anxious for this final form that the dream becomes an anxiety: a dread lest we shall find ourselves toiling toward failure or that we may die before we finish the work. But this dread is also a waywardness, and probably the only one we must forbid ourself.

Many a writing venture begins without the least prevision of the form it must somehow come to at last. Some materials and ideas are all we may have, and they beg us to work with them. And as we do so, the harder we work the less sure we may be that we're not going astray toward one fulility or another. If by dint of toil and luck, we glimpse the beginning of form in the stuff, we can then at last feel we haven't lost it, nor it us.

# Glamor and gloom

I

An irreligious artist may feel no gratitude for his gifts. He may resent them as an agony he had never elected himself to live through. But he must contain them. A gifted person is not so *un*like a holy one who has beheld a grace or a vision as to get away with any denial. The powers don't work that sloppily. That is, if one believes in them as Powers, supernal; if one doesn't, but merely as internal, they're still too potent to permit his escape. His only choice is whether or not to honor his suffering, his gift of being creative.

« »

A person of talent should be diligent in respecting it. Such respect for one's own talent is sound critical judgment.

« »

Go as humanist or neohumanist as you please, dismiss all the medieval you would, except one idea—dedication.

« »

The commitment to one's talent is not a pledge to achieve fame. Nobody has ever owed himself glory, any more than sainthood.

If secular glory takes precedence over the mystery of existence, if concern to make oneself renowned is rightly more important than a concern with the mortal session in an environment of unknownness, the need for poetry is too slight to be worth the trouble.

« »

There's never anybody else around when you wrestle with an angel.

« »

Train a child to feed on applause and he will grow up starving for appreciation. An anemia is induced in him. What he should have is rather the kind of food he helps himself to, the kind he gets when he seems to be merely playing. For his talents first appear in the form of play. Some of which will be terribly painful and make him cry.

Praise, however genuine and stimulating, is not sustenance. The artist's good food is often anything but delightful. It can be too bitter for any but an artist, who becomes one mostly through having to take it.

The sound of music is its glory; the sound of the applause is at best only a poor echo.

« »

Let's not ask for great audiences so that we may become great poets. The trouble with that longing is it gives us the habit of brooding upon the fate of our poems as much as we must on the writing of them.

If you are potentially as good a writer as you would wish, you can't afford to expend emotional energy on attentions outside your work.

This energy is so precious to some writers that they put off opening the letters they receive from their closest friends; they stint on attentions to spouse and children, who they know deserve large helpings of it. And yet with what iniquitous folly some of them will drain it away in unnecessary solicitude over public response!

« »

To write with your mind fluttering asunder from your subject because of such incentives as dreams of ovation, the sneaked-in anguishes of envy, or the smuggeries of being either in vogue or in The Tradition—all such is like inattention when driving a car. The same kinds of factors: the motor, the road, the traffic, and no insurance whatever.

« »

You can be certain that if the time should come when the public will celebrate you with splendors of laudation, nearly all of it will be for the pleasure of the celebrators. It is great fun to participate in the public's self-congratulation over your achievement—over *their* success, really, rather than yours, in recognizing what you had but effortfully glimpsed in yourself long before.

But know this now: your truest appreciation from anybody is most likely to occur within the mind of the mute, inglorious reader here and there, who is too absorbed in your work to be demonstrative about it, too respectful to importune you with personal feelings—as perhaps you too have been with some other writers. How valuable what you're now struggling to write may become to someone else to read someday, and remember and repeat, you may never know. How valuable to you it is right now for you to be writing, you do know. And may yet know better and better.

The best fame of all is silent. It must be silent, because it is taking place deep within the grateful mind, prior to articulation, much as what is meriting that fame took place originally. Count on this. It's an excellent faith.

« »

Give no heed to anthologizers, contest-stagers, juries, raters of what is first-and-second-and-third. The quality of art cannot be quantified. It cannot be calibrated. Fussers can weigh an artist's body but not his mind.

The artist who knows his business feels that it is more necessary for his work to exceed its possible rewards than for him to win them.

« »

Emulation has long been deemed the life of the classroom, in about the same philosophical key as that in which competition has been sanctified as the life of trade. It is not the life of your workroom.

« »

If you must think of your work and your world as a competition, if you must race in order to run at all, at least keep your eye on the goal your legs must reach. A good sprinter doesn't make waste motions looking back over his shoulder or to either side at his rivals. And he's no sucker for golden apples.

The competitors who seem to be grabbing off readers ahead of you may be the preparers of your audience.

« »

It's one thing to ask a publisher for large, impressive publicity; it's something else to dote on it credulously. Nothing told publicly can tell you privately how good you are. The only thing that possibly can is *perhaps* the next thing you write. Live for that very good feeling when your own work speaks back to you.

## II

Care as much about what motivates you as you do about what motivates your characters. Never permit yourself a motivation that you will be secretly ashamed of.

But your task is worthy of your humility. Only a genuine artist will choose such tasks.

« »

We must distinguish between the compulsion to say something and the divination of what needs saying. The chief impulse toward art is not a yen but a dream—the kind of dream we have when we're too awake to evade the truth.

« »

When publishers are accepting your stories and waiting for more, it's a grand feeling of buoyance and shine. When readers scattered here and there are watching for your newest poems, it's a secret feeling of serene blessedness. It's a rotten feeling when they're not.

There's another feeling deeper than these, much more serious and much less transient. It's when your *need* to say (or sing!) a certain narrative, or to bring to complete and perfect utterance a certain poetic conception, exceeds every other care. And still more than your feeling or need to write, is a poem's or story's need to be written as only you can write it. That is, you feel that its need for you alone to form it into a whole existence comports with your need to have it as an accomplishment.

« »

It's the intrinsical, intensive concern that makes for the best inceptions. When anybody, however inept and unimportant he may be, writes himself a poem or story, just so he can have it, just so he can read it in bearing, say, some ache or joy of his, a production takes place that is *authentically* prompted.

« »

Sometimes a composing gets started in us before we have any conscious wish for it. On its own initiative, seemingly, it wants to be an existent. And we must let it. Here too is an authentication. Let the piece be as unintelligible to others as it insists, it won't be mere "automatic," on-the-couch stuff so long as you have had an agreement with yourself that you've kept in private honor, to recognize the longing for form, which is immanent in any very vital notion.

« »

A writer's faith is not merely self-confidence. It's much more than a contestant's supportive bravado, the gallant boastering of ancient heroes and modern athletes—all of which you may well help yourself to as much as you need. But would-be writers and never-will-be writers lack a certain fundamental trust, and they mistake for it a conceited determination to be what they are not. Baited by glamor, they make an early vow, with scarcely anything else to go on, and their obstinate loyalty to it they substitute for that trust.

The faith of any writer as an artist is deeper-going. Not very much unlike the faith of a religious person, it is an inherent, not an imposed, incentive. This is not only the fact of being alive but the force we feel and heed toward the continuance, the furthering forth, of the life in us. Like growing up: as we pass from childhood into adolescence, and into adulthood, thence into maturity, we accept each of these stages in good faith (as though that's just what we chose to do) or else we sicken. It's a kind of humility a writer feels in his willingness to be the one that he is.

This becomes, instead of an arrogant expectation, a joyful willingness to write. The inception of his art is an assent.

« »

The word inspiration, once frequent in literary discussions, is now almost never used by writers. But the essence of what it once meant is still a vital factor. It is an impelling motor force exactly suitable for the special task.

The odd fact about inspiration, though, is that, like happiness, it is what we don't very consciously recognize until afterwards, when it seems to have passed. In most instances we don't know we're inspired when we really are. All we know is we're faced with a charge we can't get out of. And we don't want to.

« »

The reason you want to write is not a simple one. If it's any good, it's as complex as you are. Examine it as closely as you can bear to. But don't try to get it into a succinct statement. Particularly not for anybody who asks you.

Often people who appear to have some aplomb in expressiveness are asked whether they intend some day to do some writing, and they honestly reply, no, and confess that they "have no message." Such simplicity is genuine. And admirable: it honors the requirement of having a subject.

But a subject is not enough for deciding to become a writer. Ever so much else does that deciding.

« »

To the industrialist the word incentive means the prospect of increase in profits. To the artist it means what it originally did: to start in singing, strike up a tune. In the distance, or perhaps very near, there's an intimation of singing about to begin. To us an idea approaches singing. Or we awake to it.

« »

Your surest incentive for writing a poem or story is to write it just for yourself, much in the same spirit as you would have to make shelter and shoes for yourself if you inhabited a desert island alone. You do so to meet your needs. The making is likely to be very hard but the going without is sure to be still harder.

In a poet there's a certain private honesty: he may begin by allowing himself makeshifts, but after a while, they seem to be a little better for his needs than his lack of them was. He can't stand cheating himself any longer. This is nearer to a kind of selfishness than to any altruistic motivation.

Without this sense of integrity, this privily honored selfishness, your writing incentive is weakened.

*Incentive*. Not purpose. Purpose may evolve from it later. And when that happens it has a largesse which seems to have been inherent in it from the beginning.

## *Glamor and gloom*

« »

To know what it is that impels you as a writer, and to guide that impulse toward a certain kind and quality of writing, is to decide whether to make a craft or *also* an art of it.

Toward craft we train our literary skills to perform best what is required by the work at hand, and we do this under the drastic admonishments of conscience, which will not let us get away with what is merely "good enough."

Toward art we cultivate all the emotion and intellect we can summon to the service of the imagination.

Whether to be content with craft is not always for us to decide. Imagination does not always abide by such modesty. Our imagination goes past the point of our aims, though it will oftener than not, in respect for our mastery, keep in the same direction.

« »

As long as a writer, consciously or otherwise, stays within the self-expression motivational stage, he keeps himself in the kindergarten of his development. The world and all of its arts oppose anybody who is misled into believing that his self-expression is what is most needed from him.

One's entire self *does* the expressing. It is the medium, or means, of the expression, not the source or the cause of it. Or the meaning of it. Mankind does not need to have you here forever. It might, though, your poem or story.

« »

Few, cruelly few, writers have the gift of great intelligence, which is as rare as great talent and is probably the same innate virtue. But many of us with this as our shortcoming have some power to ponder on our experiences and on those of others whom we observe, and we can do this pondering with uncommon intensity, earnestness, charity, willingness to see truths, and hopefulness for a moral essence.

Out of this pondering we can form a wisdom.

Wisdom is always *formed*. It is always won out of necessities; it is never "native." It is man's work that he earn and form wisdom. Even intelligence, at its rarest brilliance, honors wisdom above itself.

« »

If it's not a story you're hankering to tell to yourself better and better until you've got it to its full bloom, it won't be quite worth the trouble to write for others—unless you're so deft at two-way deception that the slickness of the legerdemain is admired for its own sake as a form of amusement and you get paid well for it.

People pay gladly, with their "small change," for bogus experiences, such as are ingeniously frightful, lascivious, or vengeful —not solely for the impact of these but for the forgettableness of them. Much inner misery is an endless Hadean toil of forgetting. Relief, if but momentary, is preferred instead of redemption, because the restoration of one's spirit is also a labor, and it requires that kind of effort that nobody, not even a genius, can ever get used to making.

When at last you have brought your story to its full bloom, however sorrowful, the gratification lies in the keepableness of the story. To have for keeps is an equivalent of not dying.

« »

Many a could-be writer doesn't "get going" because he is like a person with a set of hobby tools and materials, who feels he ought to get busy with them but can't decide just what to make.

In the whole length of human experience the necessities came before the tools did, and we can't reverse that developmental history.

The unhappy reversal, of acquiring the means before we have experienced the meanings, is a general plight. Our young talent receives its schooling before it has felt, or without having a chance at the same time to feel, much impingement of life's other main necessities upon it. So we get into the habit of unconsciously asking: now what poem, what story, can I think up that I can use this for?

It is this condition that makes us dabble. Or become complacently decorative, or flippant, or affectedly "alienated."

« »

It is no disadvantage to be so conceited that we aim beyond our capabilities. We can't find what "beyond" is for us unless we take such a shot. An outrageous alternative we force upon ourselves will do the crippling: the writer who sets out to be "first-rate or nothing" is aiming, really, at nothing.

« »

No writer can be certain of never going adrift into the doldrums. Often unaccountably, and in such cases there is no use asking how it could have been prevented. A development of morale is possible so that one will have formed the habit of an undwindling expectation of emerging from such a plight.

This is an in-built rescue. Its development goes on every day when a writer is working either apace or haltingly. When apace, he is learning more and more the feel of expeditiousness, and he must deem this feel the same thing as faith. And when he's working haltingly, he takes the many sags and lags as they are encountered, cursing them if he likes but not himself for their occurrence.

He has accepted art and accident as being in the nature of his kind of work an undefiable combination, which has effects now blessed, now damnable, so that when he overblames himself he wastes his energy outside of the phenomenon.

There is, though, one accountable factor in the failure of many a writer who starts out with good potentiality. Sooner or later, the abject craving to achieve supreme glory turns into a sneaking anxiety about the avoidance of failure. He gets an inner tic of saying no to himself. Having too often and for too long desired the glamors of success more than the quiet (yes, even the *smug!*) realization of his latent powers and, having overlooked the special nature of his vocation with its special solaces while he was striving to master it, he has chosen his own betrayal.

Creativeness is an affirming process, and art is time and again reparative of people's spirits. What a foul irony that it should be otherwise to those who labor in it. A writer should have a fine sense of values, and yet he can be such a fool as to choose for himself the very wrongest.

## III

We must become inured to seeing other writers coming forth in print with originations that we have, perhaps for years, been wooing as ideas. If the others have done better with them than our honesty tells us we might have done, let's afford ourselves a feeling of relief from a hapless commitment. But if the same kind of honesty bids us to see that we could have done still better, let's realize that primacy isn't all, and that intimacy is more lasting. What matters in the long time ahead is not who first saw the beauty, but who married her.

« »

A fine moment in the life of a reading-writer comes when he first sees well expressed something he has often been on the verge of saying. This is almost a jealous moment; somebody else has got there first, perhaps twenty-five centuries before him. Or only a few hours, as Amundsen had before Scott. Yet, with all the rest of the world to the north of them, they alone had come to the ultimate point, and they coincided in it as closely as the meridians, their closeness to each other in this fact greater than their rivalry, out-signifying it forever.

« »

Some writers who have been famous for their genius have been also notorious for their jealousy. Their ravenousness for acclaim seems not to have impaired their greatness. (Really, we don't know whether it did or not; for all we can figure, they might have become still greater.) But the fact that there are survivors of a disease that kills almost everybody does not prove that it isn't a disease. Nor is it an argument against health to exalt the temptation to be ill. Art is a vocation, and suicide too may be a vocation. But the call for the one isn't the same as that for the other.

« »

Dogs, cats, horses, birds—all our pets, including our pet selves—can be jealous. But *we* can be also consciously creative. So when the feeling of jealousy is taking hold, often against our choosing, we have to know it for a monkey on our back, and the only way we can shake it off is to decide to resume going in any of the other directions we had been going before. Jealousy has only one direction: down into hell.

« »

As soon as a writer becomes jealous of other writers he is a lost hound. He will run yelping in many directions, barking up wrong trees.

The glamor of fame is always off the trail; it's usually floating down some boulevard where the earth is walled away from the air, along some street far from the native haunts and intimate odors of the authentic.

« »

Quit being envious of the Greats. Get on with your work.

There's no rivalry between you and the immortals. Liberate yourself to get on with your heritage. You will better feed your valor if you'll regard them as watching you with tutelary concern. They who have built our Literature, if they're still somehow somewhere around, must be watching for what more is happening to it.

For Literature is a community as much as it is a heritage. This is the respect in which the devotional study of Literature is indispensable for the growing writer. To him this study is a communion.

« »

You cannot enter where others are emerging. Go around back.

« »

When our chief, honest-to-self, reason for reading current poetry and fiction becomes watching how other writers may be getting ahead of us, the time has come for taking oneself sternly and humbly into the court of solitude to face the charges. This itself is the only punishment, and it's drastic enough. The rest is rehabilitation. And that consists of new, special enjoyments. Go in for *other* arts and endeavors, those in which you have no personal ambitions whatever but can enjoy as a layman entirely for their own sake. Relearn how to love. It may take months or a year or two. But that's how to get back to your own genuinity.

« »

At a point of coincidence between your writing and another's, you match your identity with his. Neither of you cancels the other. Any ire to do so is a weakener.

« »

Our jealousy of another writer—whether it be begrudging or emulative—forces our attention to veer from what must be his inner spirit and away also from what he, to his great benefit, has been seeing in his masters, in his and our great predecessors, and in the long history of literary striving, which is our rightful heritage as much as it is his.

« »

When you are jealous of another writer, you hate any excellence you find in him. And you rejoice over any fault, almost loving the fault for its injury to him. Both the excellence and the fault, you use as a means of his annihilation. But that doesn't happen. Instead, it's in yourself that a falling apart and a nullity may result.

But when there is no jealousy, your discovery of his fault brings you closer together, and if you can overcome it for him, this will tend to balance in you the excellence he had and you lacked. You may do all this only in your own mind. Or you may try and fail. Then you'll taste some of the pathos all writers share.

There is between writers an unwritten poem going on. The name Poet is held among them in tacit regard as being larger than any single self.

« »

Here is a story by a young writer; long ago you read it when you too were a young writer, and because he was suddenly acclaimed when you were not even noticed you were so filled with dread and enmity that the story seemed to you to be of no consequence. If any glint of merit in it caught your eye you hastily dismissed it as a poor try at what was the immense potential that you were groping toward in yourself.

But now, twenty, thirty years later you chance to come upon that story and having forgotten you had ever seen it before, you let your curiosity dally over it. It amazes you. Its simple deftness, many beautifying shocks of accurate observation, modest decencies of craft, its direct outflow from depths of prior concern, and so on: qualities in him that you may have not at that time sought in yourself and that these twenty, thirty years have been lost to you as his. He has been dead a long time now. There is no possibility of recompense to him or yourself. If he were alive he would no more need it than he does now, and there is no way for you to make it up to him, for you have been dead to his story until now and you cannot refill your past years or his.

Ah, but you may by now have achieved more than he did? That can make no difference. The loss is the same. You can only be thankful that the story has its own existence, apart from the author and his enviers. The thing that jealousy cheats us of is the same whether we are geniuses or mediocrities. For that is the way of art: to be independent of us or fade away.

« »

We ought not to deprive ourselves of feeling the amazements over achievements in the art that we profess.

There comes a time in our maturing when we realize we are beholding feats beyond our personal capability. We are free to enjoy to the full a performed surprise—free of compunction about its not being our own performance. Free of adventitious compulsion to vie with it. Then if there's anything that we do feel as a fellow-professional, it's an affinitive recognition. All true performers know just what this is: the capability of being moved as deeply as they wish to move others.

# Learning to write is learning what is yours

## I

The professional adage "nobody can be taught how to write" is not always true.

If a beginner has found he has a worth-writing, worth-reading way of utterance, there is that much evidence of a possibility of development. Only that. But at least that.

If he begins without any such intimation but with only the yen to be writer and see his words in print, if he is spellbound by the glamor of literary fame and mistakes this for inner prompting toward true vocation, he may be taught some devices to repeat, a few momentarily catchy mannerisms to imitate, and some one-two-three procedures to follow exactly. He may "get by," especially if he is a shrewd manipulator of facts or stock fancies—if he is a clever gamester, whether of the "deep" chess or the sharp poker species. But he will have only small development, hardly enough to be called that. Call it, rather, "application." Development is *growth*.

« »

To develop by oneself from the beginning, if but a little, betokens teachability. And all teaching, however expert it be, must be converted into self-teaching, if it is to become of real use to a better than ordinary writer.

They who cannot make any development after their first bright outburst are the most prone to seek instruction and are the very ones who should not. They wear out good teachers and themselves, or else become dupes of expensive, heartless "schools" that trade on the glamor bait.

« »

Some writers, for one reason or another, cannot get beyond their recognition of the first fruitful impulse. They write something very good. Then a dead stop. A misfortune, psychological or otherwise, hinders them. Often, though, the stoppage is caused by a mistake: as to just *what* in a writer is teachable. It is recognition, not impulse. To attempt to instruct impulse is to forbid it to be impulse.

Recognition is cultivable throughout one's life. Nobody taught a writer (or ever could) how to have the impulse. It simply is there. Thus blessed, he discovers it and each "first" thing he learns about how to write increases the activity of his recognitions.

« »

A writer can be taught, a writer can learn, insofar as he can imagine enhancements of his ways of rediscovering his own prime motion. Then what he performs becomes individual with him though universal in final value to others. And what is genuinely peculiar with him becomes only mannerism in his imitators: those who don't know how to be taught.

A word to the truly wise is not merely sufficient; it's exciting, abounding.

« »

It is not imperative for a producing writer to know the variations and vogues of meaning in the terms used by literary experts. He need not get into the perennial debates over what should be the correct designation of this or that function or process in the anatomy of literature. He can safely keep an oblivious detachment from the fashions in the terms which have been good words all along and still are but which suddenly appear with a frequency that seems alarming and take on a luster from the quidnuncs that never was needed.

What is imperative is that he have an instinct, a propensity, an experiencing savvy, an operative familiarity, about the functions and processes denoted by those terms even though he does not know the terms themselves. He may have chosen his own designations or "handles," or he may have not bothered to do even that. But the processes themselves will be as familiar to him as the range and modulations of his own voice.

To have someone think he must tell you that what you have been working for anyhow is "the objective correlative" is like his presuming you will be surprised to learn that what you have been speaking all your life is prose.

« »

The person who has the writing aptitude (which is more than an inclination) may forget the very instructions of which he is in most need. If he is disinclined to write, despite the actuality of his talent, that will be that. (It may be just because he has talent, and its presence terrifies him, that he cannot bring himself to write—his intuitions surmise the travail, the dread knowledge of the life in the offing, and so he shuns instruction.) If he complies with his talent (and this deep-seated *willingness* to write—to suffer, to behold, to come across with, to be ever and again unthanked—is rarer than talent), his concern with it becomes his guide. Like a planet keeping its orbit because the centripetal force is not less than the force of the outward swing, he feels that his inner resources are constantly magnetic to his attentions, and his outer resources seem to come to him because of the same inner attraction.

There is only one way in which he can avail himself of valuable instruction: instead of looking upon it as proffered teaching added from another's talent and experience to his own, he must look upon its substance as kindred matter, affinitive with him; he must regard its advent as a truth (or a truing) that he already knows, and as a skill that had already been forming in him.

« »

The criticism your instructor offers may be ever so valid and your feeling about it ever so agreeable, but unless it triggers an activity, a freshness of hope, an improved outlook—unless you feel alacrity in applying it, it is not likely to work.

This appropriation happens seldom among writers. We have here probably the chief reason why editors and other advisors are prone to believe (secretly) that "it's no use—authors can't learn."

Why does it happen so seldom? Perhaps each writer must find his own answer. The chances are the answer will emerge in that quarter in which his enthusiasm for writing has its rise. If he is one of the legion who only want to be writers, to see themselves seen as such, and who for solely that reason go to work, it will not be writing, itself, he truly cares about. He may have plenty of zeal but it is for the career and not the art; the art itself as an exertion is but a wan metonymy with him for the posture, the simulation, the career.

Only one other thing can advantageously interest the learning writer as much as the art itself, and that is his *subject*. This is much closer to the art, more germane to it, than is any aspect of the career. In fact, career and the art are two very different and separate things, and usually have so little to do with each other that as often as not the relation between the two is ironical. But the subject takes to the art and the art to the subject in somewhat the same affinitive manner as the artist and his instructor take to each other.

## II

What the literary historians include in their studies and surveys ought not to be of much concern to the working writer who deals with his subject imaginatively. Their tasks and his have but little similarity. They are always making their progress in a direction the reverse of his, proceeding from his goal back to his outset, conducting recursions of what were for him excursions, often uncharted. Their attitudes must needs be after the fact, however much and honorably they intend their study to coincide with the before-the-fact position. Although historifying can invite rather than suppress the scholarly imagination, and although historians are sometimes more imaginative in dealing well with actual events than some putatively creative writers are in dealing with any kind of event, the literary historians cannot help you in *writing* your story or your poem.

Aestheticians may speculate and expatiate on the sense of beauty and on what constitutes the work of art, as an "object," and you may read their theories with the elation of having come across some affable minds; critics may make points with gleaming precision that you would emulate, and they may be as articulate about a literary process as you long to be about your own subject. Yet you will not receive in perhaps months of reading such works one truly relevant intimation of your own writing aptitude. Their minds are in an occupational posture which becomes more and more fixed as they advance in expertness about consummations, typal masteries, tendency detections, etc., and so their imagination gets less and less exercise in the incipient phases of the phenomenon of writing.

« »

The problem of instruction is not that of what school or tradition or anti-tradition a young writer should take up. The problem is the modern predicament of miscellaneity everywhere affecting everyone. Paradoxically, this mix goes along with the commercial monotonies, the mechanical mores, and the political conformisms.

In such a world the young artist should be likened to a good hound, and the most important part of his education is to be put on the right scent. He may find it by himself or never find it unless someone else has a way of wandering around with him until they come across the scent that is his to pursue. His imagination must have a nose. He must keep nosing here and there and yon until he finds the scent that puts all of him into action: a line of action, fading and tortuous perhaps, but continuous. Essential as all the rest of his education is (the masterpieces, languages, rhetoric, and philosophies, and the sciences), it decreases in importance as it keeps him off this scent, and increases only as it gives him the stamina and the keenness to to his hounding.

We already anticipate the experience in our realizing that the most effective instruction we ever receive only serves to remind us of what we feel we have somehow known before.

But the scent itself is also something more: a *subject*. A subject that you know for your own. If you feel yourself spontaneously owning to it within the depths of your animate self, you can be sure you are on the right scent. Go to it, and with it.

The danger is that you might disown it because it seems too slight or because it seems too grand. Either way, such a denial is as calamitous as repudiating your creative spirit.

To deny your subject is to deny your vocation.

As you and your subject continue to work on each other, there will be a unique compatibility between you.

What will be called your style will inhere in this. It is the only true style possible for you, and precisely because it is inseparable from you-on-the-right-scent it is distinctive among all the other styles. Learning to write is learning what is yours.

« »

There are a great many writers who "have everything": talent, education, taste, sophistication, seclusion, plenty of time and health—everything except a subject. And if they have that, it's one they "got": acquired, picked up. It's not really theirs, and they don't know how to make it theirs. For it's no easier to do so than to make a spouse your very own. So they fall sadly short of their promise.

A subject becomes yours when it especially needs you, when you can believe, in the silent privacy of your own mind, that you alone have some certain feeling or touch or insight or foresight or temper or tone or God-and-you-know-what-else that it can receive from nobody but yourself. It may be a hard one but it will teach you how to write.

## III

To discover one's own knack, one must accept one's self, as we must our height and skin. But one's self is an immense maze of contiguities, and there is no telling specifically what interest or quirk that has no apparent connection with one's unformed skill may nonetheless lead into it. For example, a violinist may explain his concert virtuosity by saying, "I always put on old clothes and take a bus ride out to the gasworks and walk around." It seems crazy, or superstitious. It is neither. It is a unique consistency which belongs to that person. It is his private switch that connects within him the precise elements required by his performance. We must not be afraid of appearing quixotic.

« »

Sometimes a story has a similarity to the rather simple satisfactions of a melody, with its intimations and promises, its momentary suspenses, its changing fulfilments (some of which are tentative), and probably most of all, its character as a varying continuum. This latter feature is so certain an element that a child hearing a melody for the first time can notice a failure in that aspect. Likewise noticeable to him is the comparable failure in a story. A writer who can't figure out what may be wrong with his story-making should find this analogy suggestive.

Nearer to actual story-making practice is the training one can get out of telling (rather, *re*telling) anecdotes and jokes to improve them. Now, admittedly, a serious literary narrative is no joke, but still there are small formal features that both share. Although the "effect" we try for in a joke or an anecdote is quite different from what we might try for in a short story or a novel, there is considerable kinship in the inconspicuous provisions that give almost any kind of narrative a boost. Here are some:

> Touching the imagination soon enough with a concrete detail so that it is picturable. Making certain that either this imagined "picture," or another, figures somehow for an impingement in the ending. Be an imagist for this; use a potent image.
>
> Some strategy in the precedence and sequence of the details so as to build up. In inept tellings the ordering is haphazard so that a detail that should come later is brought in too soon and vitiates the interest in the succeeding details, or else an earlier detail is skipped ("Oh, I forgot to say that—") and the later mention ends the submission of the listener to the narrator.
>
> Keeping just enough build-up so that the narrative builds continuously, and no more.
>
> Sensitizing the listener for the finale, particularly by being astute in the minding of your connotations; avoid any that might desensitize him.
>
> Minding your emphases. Keeping to the fewest. Spacing them at suspenseful distances, in a strategic rhythm. Avoiding misemphasis. What comedians call "timing" is usually

a control of emphasis: its best placements, where and how long the pauses. In writing, these pauses have an equivalent in the lengths of sentences, phrases, and even of words.

Practice in retelling anecdotes and jokes can be as helpful a training as any writing exercises, which may perhaps become tedious. To be sure, some of the finest fiction writing can do without the proficiencies suggested above; but the writer who is troubled by lacking a "sense of story" will find it is not too mystical to achieve, if he tries this "practice."

« »

In any work in which imagination prefigures, all instruction that is valid is special, specific, and tentative. By learning from the ways of others, an artist risks being obedient, given to affectation and modishness, stereotyping, and inhibition; by depending upon his own resources, he risks being chaotic, foolishly arbitrary, spuriously mystical, and dismally silly. Yet he must take both risks. The worst risk of any is to choose one of these *instead* of the other. If you are becoming as good as you hope to be, only complete safety is dire.

« »

How it is done. How to do it. The difference between these two how's is fundamental. Where there are a thousand who know how it is done, there will be only one who knows how to do it. *They* can tell you *their* how: the information is purchasable at many schools and in many manuals. But he cannot tell you *his*. He often wonders about it, almost in the same way as the instruction-seeker does who tries to probe him. But the audacity of this attempt startles him, for he dare not so probe himself. He may think, and say, that it just happens, and yet he cannot tell how he is able to work so extremely hard, and why he must, during that self-formative event.

## IV

It is doubtful that revelatory legends have come into being wholly through individual authors. Nearly all these (however special any of them might seem to be in structure and style) must have developed through a long succession of recitations during many generations. Although there must have been in each case a very first, original utterance of it, this is unlikely to have occurred *ex nihilo*. Some object or animal or scene or event or spirit was very probably credited for it, or for the suggestion of it, by the author in his own mind.

But regardless of how convincingly modern research may prove such an attribution—that is, point to a prior stage or form or model—the utterer was an expressionist. And each time a modification of the received version took place, the impetus for that was a functioning of expressionism. Something happens within the user of a tradition, especially if he is an *impassioned* user and not a mechanical user of it, that expands the utterance as such. If it occupies his consciousness at all, he will fill into it more color and depth of tone. The whole-hearted user of a given mode of expression or tradition is in line to become one of its contributing authors.

When we have thought through this matter we are prepared to deal with the more-or-less academic proposition that the way to learn how to write is to study and imitate the proper models.

A pun is necessary here: this counsel depends on what the learner *makes* of the model. There is a difference between making the same kind of thing and making something out of that thing. There's a difference between making out of the model a static or a dynamic fact. The *presence* of originality itself may be a moot question but the *impulse toward* a possible originality either is or is not an actuality. A teacher who has lost or who has never experienced this impulse is worse for a writer than the absence of any teacher or models.

« »

If you learn a poem by heart and develop a way of saying it better and better, you will likely find riches in it *and in yourself* responding to them that you had not dreamed of. The same will happen if you copy the poem in your own handwriting and do so because you like that poem and because you find this to be a good way of being with it and having it with you. This is not at all the same "exercise" that may have been imposed upon you in school. Few teachers know how to lead anybody into intimacies.

No doubt many good writers, in the Occident and in the Orient, have used models in their early training. Did they in their later development abide by those models? To find this out you may have to be a scholar, but will have to be still more of a writer. For the *potency* of a model is its efficacy to a growing writer. It must suffuse him with its spirit; he must feel the spell of it. If this happens imitation will not content him; he will not be satisfied until he has caught the momentum of it and is impelled toward expression. As its author was. Forcefully. The same empowerment goes on. If he feels *that*, he will have outdistanced his teacher. And perhaps his venerated master too.

# Definitions: their sterility

Play with definitions if there is fun in them for you, but do not try to work with them.

In technology and in military training, definitions have a practical function; they fence in the meaning that must be used and they fence out all other meanings. When a science teacher or an artillery instructor says, "This definition will prevent error," he is implying, sagaciously too, that it forbids imagination. Or invention, or originality of any kind whatever. The purpose of a definition is to fix a judgment so that it will stay fast and provide an adamant datum for sharp precision. It is as anti-creative a gadget as man has ever contrived.

Many academic teachers of writing have adopted the martinetism of the military, especially in the textbooks they pound and rivet together and then try to use. Their reasons though, for requiring definitions are not the same as those of the engineering professor; they merely do not know any more than anybody else does just how someone can learn how to write, and so a definition of what poetry or a novel is supposed to be saves them from embarrassment.

« »

In the universities, if literary students ask for definitions, there are two reasons. One is that definitions will be asked of them in the examinations by professors who have no other way of knowing what a student has "learned," because they know too little to teach that which cannot be thus examined. The other reason is that the definition-craving student wishes to know by having an abstraction what he is unwilling to know, or incapable of knowing, by feeling, which is essentially suffering. (Even when joyousness is there.) Experiencing, which is the immediate way of learning, is the most formidable way. The people who can never really know what poetry (or art, or beauty, or truth, or even democracy) is are the ones who are forever demanding definitions of it. They read and read *about* it, acquiring more and more "clearly defined ideas" of it, all the while *knowing* it less and less.

To you, a writer, such people may be of no concern, except that they become reviewers and critics (less often, editors) and they do their job as though they were reading examination papers. If your poem, or short story, or novel, or play, or essay does not contain some evidence that you know and respect their definitions, they will grade (*rate*) you accordingly. There is also a reading public equipped with definitions, probably not remembered word-by-word but operative anyhow as subconscious Geiger counters for "appreciation," and you have to put up with them too. That is, you have to allow for their existence, and then go on having your own not one least bit the less.

« »

The moment you are satisfied with a definition of a poem or a story, you have substituted the writing of it, and had better not go on to write it, unless you enjoy the profligacy of such wasted motion.

There is such a thing as a definition that is creative. Or, since it is an act rather than a statement, we might better speak of it as creative defining.

You know pretty definitely what it is you wish to do. That is, at the outset, or in the midst of the work, or afterwards, you have a definite notion or feeling of what you wish the poem or story or play to be. More than that, what the poem or story or play, itself, wishes to be. This takes a world of *savoir-faire*, and only you, the only author of this one piece of work, can know that definition.

« »

Vague people are prone to make a merit of vagueness. They refuse to see definiteness. Even when it is necessary, they reject it because its recognition calls for intellectual effort and they believe a limp intellect is a limber one.

But to demand definiteness where it is impossible is also a kind of vagueness.

Both kinds of people are usually opinionated, and opinionated people detest everybody's perverseness but their own.

« »

We do not ascertain our existence by definition when we take a bite of food or give a kiss. We are all the more certain of it without a definition.

« »

Both definitiveness and vagueness can become obsessive in any kind of creative activity.

Art must not tarry awaiting proof and definition of its existence, or even a nice sensible examination of it.

If you feel need for thankfulness for God, go ahead and pray without proof or definition. Do the same with poetry: get to work.

« »

A sedulous mind may compact a "working" definition of a poem. But not a working one of poetry. Only a tentative, suggestive one that "leaves the rest to the imagination." And never any least possible definition of a poet.

To define a poem—to answer the question, What is a poem?—is to form perhaps a more specific statement than you might in defining poetry, but it will be no less a fatuity for the prospective enjoyer or maker of poems. The more defining it may appear to be, the less potentiality is there for any poem which a reader or writer may anticipate with that definition. (If a reader applies that definition to a specimen he has already examined without it, he will be only "checking on" the work, trying somewhat mechanically to see if it matches, and his very act of decision, either way, fastens him to irrelevancy.)

Each poem originates in the same predicament as was that of the first poem ever made: it has for itself only the intimation of its *coming* into being, not the imperative to repeat being. It forms itself precariously. This is just as true of a sonnet or a triolet as of an unfixed form of verse.

The best we can do is to write a poem that has intent and fulfils it, and does so by holding itself together as a sufficient whole—all this in its own unique way, with a relish of its content as if in defiance of all definitions, even the one it would seem to make of itself. This is what you might advisably feel before you write it as much as while you write it. Like a lover who dreams ahead and then discovers the entirety of his anticipations only through realizing them.

« »

To enjoy living among the productions of human beings, or not impair that enjoyment, the foremost admonitions to ourselves should be to quit asking, Is it poetry? Is it art? No matter how irrefutable we may believe our notion of either to be, the very presence of that notion as a proviso in the forepart of our mind becomes a block. It weakens our enjoyment of the proffered object, even when that object suits that definitive preconception.

A conscious criterion is importunate if we place it on guard duty at the gateway of our sensibility. Before we can enter into the poem (writing or reading it) this guard stops us for identification and we miss the indispensable start of the performance.

Is this poetry? Is this art? Is this love? As soon as you have asked this, it no longer is, and you're outside, in the cold.

« »

If you can't decide whether to make a poem of it or to put it into prose, neither you nor it may be ready. Wait.

There's wasteful waiting and there's germinative waiting. It's the difference between incourageous postponement and expectant patience.

When you and it are ready for each other, your writing it down will do the deciding; poetry has its own kind of impulse—unmistakable, for it is insistent and refuses to be prose. If it doesn't sing lyrically it will at least cantilate, ponderingly perhaps or morosely or burningly, under your breath or under your hand. Prose just speaks, says it out. Not without its talky rhythm and its changes of pitch. It may have a faint yearning to be poetry, not enough for compromise but sufficient for charm. Prose is too strongly itself for any doubting.

« »

In the entire vocabulary of philosophy, of theology, or of sociology the easiest word for us to define is "evil". Evil is the enemy of love. Simply that. But "love" is not definable. Likewise "truth" and "beauty."

What has this to do with writing? Everything. Especially with fiction. And here we have the innermost, most germinal secret pith of the seed of fiction: evil is ever at pains to define each of these unfenceable ideas. So every story (though not every poem!) is an account of the strife between evil and love or love's allies, the other two undefinables.

And evil is always the aggressor. (Love spreads without aggression, and contracts without diminution.)

Evil may in the end prevail *in the story* but not in the universe, which (for us) has no end: evil cannot put love out of existence. Nor does love aim to annihilate evil, either within or outside of fiction: it just continues to exist however much evil may toil to interrupt or destroy that existence. Love does not render evil ineffectual: in the long, eternal run, evil renders itself ineffectual in its siege against love.

But this self-frustration of evil is not always, or even often, the stuff of story. Much oftener, evil has *moments* of effectuality. Such a moment may be a day or an era. It is out of these moments that we get the kinds of fiction we call realism, naturalism, existentialism. Thus the strife is something much more considerable than a scrap between the bad guys and the good guys. (In fact, many of the most brilliant story-writers do not know how much more this can be: they seem complacent in their success of making little else than a gimmick of evil's effectuality, which can be only momentary, just as they make also a gimmick of death.)

Evil in disguise seeks to define love, beauty, truth. This is what makes for story. But the result is only that in turn, evil is itself defined. This is the aftereffect of story, great story.

# Advantageous difficulties

## I

It is in those difficulties that sometimes make you despair of being a genuine artist that you may discover your originality.

As an artist, you are as much the result of your ineradicable irregularities as you are of your cultivated precisions.

This is not an affair of becoming "reconciled" to irregularities. It is, rather, a self-befriending inclination to make use of them. One doesn't have to become reconciled to his thumbprints. They simply identify him. They're useful because they are irregularities. And as such, they're unique.

« »

Some of your faults you should not try to get rid of, or to hide. Instead, examine them closely and a bit tenderly. You may find use for them, and if not exactly that, their presence within you might indicate some quality or knack hitherto unavailable because it was hidden from your skimming consciousness.

« »

What we have to say may be beyond our present ability to say it. We are than facing the intellectual predicament of persistently enterprising *Homo sapiens:* the most valuable answer he can find to a serious question will carry him to a further question. But it makes him move on. Question is power.

A good sailor uses the winds more for their power than for their direction. He cannot blow but he can steer, and what he dreads is the lack of any winds rather than their contrariness.

« »

Our imagination may exceed our articulateness. If we are courageous we go on imagining anyhow, staggering toward utterance.

Because poetry finds new things to say through its struggle in the saying, the utterance sometimes exceeds our ability to understand it.

And understanding, if we achieve it, is still another advance in the saying. Some poetry stays in force through the generations because it gives our minds no rest.

The *writing* of it keeps going on and on in the readings. Only a minority of readers, some of them writers, care to participate in this process. But this is really *the* way, if any there be, in which great audiences make great poets.

« »

A faithful poet will not abandon a subject or an idea because of its difficulty. The poetic imagination takes an interest in that very difficulty, *as a difficulty*.

The uniqueness of a subject may be brought out, thanks to the uniqueness of its difficulty.

If for all his effort the poem (or story) is still difficult for him to understand, better to have it obscure than for him to be oblivious. Better to fail in articulating understandably than to evade and forget. This is a poet's secret valor. He will not use anaesthesia against the agony of utterance.

« »

In the arts, understanding is a formative process. We *form* an understanding, and we understand by achieving form. This is why form can be called "significant."

As an artist works with the form of what he is trying to produce he is giving it what is for him its best intelligibleness.

The painter's hand thinks and his mind paints. The hand writes thinkingly and the mind thinks writingly. Not readingly, at this early stage.

The writer must write toward an understanding, as later the reader will read toward it. People who are intolerant of this process have no call to be reading imaginative literature, let alone trying to write it.

« »

Because of the tragic nature of life and therefore of the predicament in which a serious writer must work, much of the process of writing is done in hell. He must go down to retrieve his soul: his "identity," self-containment, stride. Both the visit to hell and the emergence from it are extremely difficult. What makes excellence rare is not the rarity of talent but the dearth of the valor needed for the faring.

« »

If you cannot produce suspense in a story, or are always missing opportunities for the inherent suspense, the likelihood is that you are afraid of what drama you may find for it. You back away from the drama and then are in the darkness of the difficulty of perceiving it. But, more than that, you may be reacting with extraordinary dread of it because its very power is extraordinary.

« »

Almost in the same way as our dreams sometimes annoy us by importuning us with twisty problems when we are disarmed in the privacy of our sleep, the dream we are in when we are writing will often turn up difficulties that are torment. Much of the work of writing is a toilsome wakeful dream.

The seeming "troubles" of these moments are not wholly afflictions, nor always such; sometimes they are supplies. This "writing-dreaming" mind may make confusion while bringing thematic goods to us. The difficulty here is that we have to be hospitable to all this so that we can have any of it. Once we have it at hand, right on paper before our eyes and not crowding forth from our minds, we can handle it: discern the relevancies and dismiss the useless. And perhaps make out some unexpected meanings.

One or two of these meanings may be so horrifyingly difficult to deal with (phrase accurately, carry safely, etc.) that if we had foreseen it early enough, we'd probably never have tackled the poem or story we're writing. It's because of this dread in us that our "dream" tricks us with its furtive cunning.

« »

As children learn by advancing from tiny successes, they help establish the principle of purposive change. A major development takes place when a child learns by advancing from failures, his own and those of others. This engenders an interest in the discovery of difficulties as indications of creative possibilities.

« »

Knowing one's own inner authority and developing the right skill to go with it would probably not be so difficult if one could have grown up within a neatly compact culture which was safely rooted in the place where one abides, or if one nomadically carried such a culture as a sacred possession while forever traveling in search of the same kinds of grass and meat that stick to one's ribs. Such a place would be a writer's village or camp in which he has lived so long that it has become, through absorption, himself and it lives—actually abides vivaciously—within him. Likewise his universe would become his village. He would hardly have to discover and choose his mode of thought, prophecy, or song, for if ever he did, the mode would most likely ensue from the same prayers he had always known.

It is another matter when you must start from scratch that you are not sure is scratch to conceive your own prayers that you are not sure of either. Much of the difficulty of modern writing originates here. The writer cannot often overcome enough of the difficulty to avoid passing it on to the reader. (It even becomes the very theme of the song or story or sermon.) Is it then any wonder that there is in our writings a tendency toward pretentiousness, affectation, mannerism? Or to avoid this, toward stylelessness and sophisticated crudeness? Or a tendency toward fashionable tendencies?

We must, therefore, dress down our indictments before bringing our miscreant selves into our court of conscience.

« »

Just as there are fake antiques there are fake villages.

Many writers settle for what they believe to be ultimate simplicities. "Honesty" becomes a slogan. A piece of work or of non-work, becomes justifiable because it is "honest," if nothing else.

Sooner or later, the villaging of one's ways of art turns out not to be simple. One can no more conjure a true village to "move in on" than one can fabricate an age to be reborn in.

## II

Writing is not simply the result of thinking; it is also a way of thinking.

In a mathematical cogitation, the writer of the symbols is thinking *with* the writing of the symbols. They are active parts of his thought process. At any given moment in this process he may not know whether he is "saying" anything or not. Or, if he is, just what.

This is a productive affair primarily, not merely an affair of transmission.

"Communication" is a word with which readers browbeat writers. To require of a writer that he should not write except to communicate is to ignore the phenomenon of literary production. Would you say that a scientist who is examining an organism is communicating? A writer does much writing to examine.

Some of this cogitative, examining writing he does is valuable to him in itself. And to other writers, who wish to fare through the same process. And to nonwriters who want to see what this process is.

« »

The imaginative writer's inceptive concern is with the difficulties of conceiving formations rather than with the probable difficulties of reading.

Critics analyze a writer's primary difficulties in order to understand the nature of Literature, and not merely the particular piece of writing under analysis. But a writer must study the nature of his difficulties in order to produce a literature that rewards examination.

In understanding their nature, he does not so much excuse himself for not having overcome them as to provide himself with patience in meeting charges of obscurity by readers who do not realize that what they are at times blaming him for is really not his failure but his audaciousness in coming up against so great a difficulty at all.

« »

Willing though some readers may be to grant that the *gift* of writing is a mystery to them, they are not likely to allow for the continuance of the mystery beyond this.

« »

Much has been published to explain to readers why imaginative literature is often difficult to understand. Where those difficulties of the reader coincide with the author's, we have something to gain from such explanations. The better the reader's skill the more likely is his trust that what he reads with difficulty was even more difficult to write. (Also the more surely can he detect an instance of what was made too hard for him by the author's having made it too easy for himself!)

« »

## *Advantageous difficulties*

There is a kind of obscurity that a writer feels is a challenge not alone to his own imagination but to mankind's.

It may be an unforeseen clarity.

Be it an obscurity or a clarity that rings true* with him, he feels its affinity for men at large. His peculiar ingenuousness assumes that no person who is conscious is wholly without imagination. A pittance of it must be counted upon by him. And anybody who values his own consciousness is potentially a poet, a fellow poet. All this is assumed tacitly by the very act of speaking out as a writer: by publishing, in the very urge to utter.

« »

To bring meaning out from its hiding, to redeem an idea from darkness—these are services enough for practical writing, and they may require considerably more thinking ability and writing ability than is exercised by the usual textbook of the mechanics of expository writing, but they are not enough for the kind of writing that transcends its utility.

« »

There is considerably more to poetic lucidity than ordering in a clear arrangement the mess of most people's thinking and even the chaos of thought inevitable in rare, venturesome minds.

Since the word lucidity itself is a metaphor, we may work it further by thinking of a dazzling, momentarily *blinding* light. Poetic lucidity is an epiphany, and an actual epiphany is wonder-

*"Ring true" is a good test-phrase for poetry. The "true" may suffice for practical expression but the "ring" is what is required for the poetic. To get this ring takes that "knowing-together" from which we have the concept and the word "conscience."

striking. It demands a new effort of apprehension. Instead of making things easier, it offers a new difficulty. Lazy minds do not want the lucid. They want only a repetition of what their eyes are already used to.

« »

It is poetry's nature to face that darkness which nothing else will enable us to look at, let alone see into, *so early* in human experience.

Dawn is a principal working-notion for poetry: early light. The poet has been the Dawn Boy not only for the American Indian but for all the cultures that have had poetry.

« »

Most of the wrangle of poetry versus science (their differences and conflicts and similarities and affinities) is profitless to the imaginative writer, who can go in deep for both. He is likely to nose into anything, anyhow. One fact, however, in this wrangle is significant to him, and certain: that poetry often anticipates science and is not replaced by it. No matter how much science he learns he is always a poet first, just as poetry came first in mankind's story and is still coming first.

« »

If now and then a poem did not exceed the poet's notion of what he is saying, there would be no poetry. There would be only jingles and jangles, lusty preachings, diverting sentimentalizations, and so on, enough to stock a literary emporium. But no poetry.

Poetry passes over and through the customary horizons and disappears from the sight of shore-fastened minds that cannot believe the distance is not a flat one with an edge off which the exceeders fall out of existence, down into nothingness.

Poetry is not required to be knowledge so new that it seems abstruse. Nor strange, outlandish. Instead, it is that in which we feel a new capacity for knowing. It is that in which we continue to be all that we have been, and with cumulative energy of consciousness. In this continuance is also a propulsion. The only genuine newness we can be sure of in our universe is that which in ourselves is renewable: our potential.

As writers, we find our best difficulties there.

## III

There is for a writer no fruitful advantage in passing on to his readers any difficulty or deficiency of his with which he bluffs them into doing for him what he is too lazy, inept, or pretentious to do for himself.

« »

A poor writer will mistake a meagerness of significance for a difficulty in reaching any. In all walks of life, and not alone in the subtle arts, significance is more elusive than style. Many a deficient writer has contrived the semblance of a style that disguises his poverty of significant substance, and we must not let ourselves feel he is surpassing.

« »

A true artist knows himself as much by the kind of failures he prefers as by the kind of successes.

« »

Without intending to reach *a* meaning, an author may as well not set out. It is not so much an India as an India-route, not so much an aim as a hope richer than the known aim. What he may come to he may misname, but it will be THERE. There! There! He longs to have his mind exclaim it.

He may or may not know what he means. Or he may write what is clear to him and also will be for his readers, and yet it may not be the meaning after which he is hankering.

He has a scarcely conscious and yet probably deeply founded notion that if *he* should understand the meaning of his completed poem or story better than anybody else ever will, the chances are that *it* may not have enough meaning to be worth surviving him. (Always there is ever so much to be meant.)

He may or may not yet know what he *can* mean. One of the few rare but secret signs that he has the mind of an artist is that he doesn't always know what it is he is looking for until he finds it. This procedure seems fatuous to methodical people who have a method precisely to avoid emergencies and emergents, *both;* but it is the only sure way an imaginative thinker, let alone a writer, can make a *go* of it. To mean, he must go. There is no alternative.

« »

The conscientious* obscurity is one the dauntless writer feels as a challenge not alone to his own imagination but to mankind's: to

*Let us remind ourselves that "conscience" and "consciousness" are etymologically but different pronunciations of the same word.

the imagination itself as an authentic power. His vocation necessitates a consciousness so wide and deep that people who cannot devote zeal to the enlargement of their own must refer to his when they need to exceed their routine.

(Good critics afford him an attendance to his conscience but they cannot supply him with one.)

If your honesty as a writer is steady you will have your readers trusting what you say when that becomes too hard for them, as it was for you, to understand.

« »

An imaginative writer cannot afford to hide anything, for if he does he will fall into the habit of hiding from himself. He must be too astute to hide either his impossibilities or his art. Both of these situate themselves just where they belong, if the work is honest. No deceptions are at work, toward his readers or back toward him.

« »

The nature of difficulty is such that there is among thoughtful people a feeling of respect for it. We only make humbugs of ourselves if we trade on this feeling by fabricating unwarranted difficulties. Such as: factitious symbolism, snidely withheld information, puzzlework patterns of supposed connotations, fragmentary presentations which affect an air of portentousness or of vast implication.

« »

There is the kind of reader who is afraid to admit, even to himself, that he doesn't "get it." He likes to believe he takes this or that abstruseness as a compliment to his intelligence. There is also the kind of writer who caters to this species. This traffic in ostentatious difficulties can become a bustling racket.

« »

The honestest kind of honesty has no sales value, is unexhibitable and uncheckable, but has a function that feeds back and forth between the artist and his art, the workman and his work. Tell a thorough workman—the kind that built the medieval cathedrals—that what he is so conscientious in doing will never be seen on the outside; tell him that nobody will ever know about it, and he will reply, "*I* will."

It is this kind of honesty that counts with the artist, who may be a rascal who will filch your liquor, steal your spouse, borrow your money and forget, cheat in poker—all this with no compunctions whatever. His aesthetic honesty though, is his very being. An unembarrassable integrity. It is what he adds to the art even though he may make no other contribution.

« »

A fine reward for encountering our genuine difficulties in good spirit, whether they be inherent or incidental, whether thus within ourselves or in our task, is a special ease.

It is an ease like that of singing. The utterance does come out, seemingly emerging on its own power. To others this may seem effortless, but to us it is a congeries of many kinds of effort, and what we feel as ease is that our efforts have now become congruent. Everything now comes intact and goes together.

We may have failed to solve a central problem or to achieve a complete illumination. Yet that ease is a joy.

# Interest

I

Why do some writers succeed in attracting and holding the interest of readers, and other writers fail? Fail though equally deserving?

Inside and outside of writers generally, there are a great many factors active in a great many varying combinations, so that it is only by chance that a working writer might espy in a diligent survey of them a tip he can take for his own prosperity.

His interest in the problem of interest is ordinarily a concern with facilities and difficulties peculiar to himself. Yet, if he is in trouble, he must make that survey as if he weren't: that is, he must do it objectively, like a student. His danger then is like that of a medical student in symptomatology, particularly the fellow who isn't feeling quite well himself. But go through with it he must. It can't become as bad as his neglect of the problem.

« »

There's the knack of attracting attention and there's the skill of holding interest. We must have both. We must not mistake the one for the other. Today the life-tone of mercantilism has got into too much of almost everybody's consciousness. Advertising, headlining, "featuring" pervade our style of thought and our manner of presentation so that far too many a poem or story is entirely an attention getter and nothing as an interest holder. There's no failure more detrimental to the writer privately than the one that was for a while publicly a success.

« »

A distinguished writer had been importuned by an aspirant to read the manuscript of the latter's novel, but somewhere in the middle of it had quit reading. "I can't go on. You are not really interested in your story."

And the author wasn't! He was interested instead in showing what he could do with some technical features about which the brilliant critics at that time were making much serious discussion.

Here, thus, is the inside vital of the seed: the *author's own interest* in his *story*. (Or poem.) It is the first, the fundamental, often the only necessary element for eliciting a reader's interest.

In most instances it is what a writer prays for, rather than "inspiration." And it does not come about by being waited for. It is generated, produced. It is *had*.

The interest that vitalizes a story or poem must at first be our very own without the least bit of concern as to whether it is also anybody else's.

This very-ownness is the good reason why writers tend to be autobiographical in their early efforts, seizing upon and holding on to experience special to themselves—special in quality, connotation, and import. They may not be able to figure out exactly what the import is; they may feel that a symbolism is there, without being certain of just what. But this is not an obscurity for them, because they are thoroughly interested. Somewhere, somehow this is with them a generative force. It moves in the work toward the making of the story or poem, rather than in the writer toward the task of making a try for fame.

« »

What, *exactly what*, would you earnestly wish to say even if you had no literary gift and skill to put to use, and no literary aspirations? What, just what, anger do you long to tell out just for yourself to hear? And just what beauty? To behold it before you? To know it for itself?

« »

Merely to be articulate is enough if you have interest. An ignorant, untalented person with a grievance or an ecstacy or a discovery or a pity or a thing to laugh about will write, if he's articulate, a more appreciable piece than anyone else might who is loaded with talent, skill, and material but lacking in *intrinsical* interests.

« »

Are you trying to find and work out a story-idea in order to make use of the techniques, devices, fiction theories, etc. you have lately acquired? Or have you already a story-idea that is undeveloped and for which you are seeking among these acquired tools and knacks the right ones to develop and present that story? This decides whether you are a dabbler in, or a writer of, fiction.

Are you trying to figure what to do with a white elephant on your hands, or are you trying to ride a bucking Pegasus?

## II

No poet is only a poet. Each is much besides and that is a poet's threshold, his access to his poetry and his readers' access to his poems. Much could-be poetry is inaccessible simply because the authors, in their attempt to have it "far out" or "objective" have removed the threshold.

« »

To a poet the question of how to have interest—feel it and afford it—is about the same as asking how to have a spiritual experience.

No writer of exploratively imaginative fiction or poetry can hope to be interesting unless he directs his energies—perhaps unconsciously—*toward* spiritual experience, no matter how zealously he may profess disbelief in such. It must be toward rather than away from, and deep in his mental workings, whatever variety of positivism he may do his philosophizing with.

The fact is, whether or not existence is "absurd," that affair of our mind we name as "spiritual experience" is something we long for the more conscious we are of being alive. It is probably a hunger for meaning, certainly a fundamental hunger in the so-called psychic part of our nature. The best tip a writer can have on the process of being both interested and interesting is this hunger.

« »

The stories you hunger to read again and the poems that seem to gratify some need when you repeat them from memory or reread them, take these as your reminders of *how it feels to be interested.*

Among the pieces we do not hunger to reread, we can reasonably suspect that many were written perfunctorily rather than hungrily, or only as determined efforts to awaken zest when there was not hunger, only a feeling of obligation to act as though it were there.

But interests vary. Admitting that, let us continue with the idea of "hunger," or need, as a factor in the problem of interest.

Find, feel the need. Intuit it, guess it, gamble on it. Above all, get into the actuality of the experience of the need. Your need or the public's, or perhaps, with good luck, both.

Search for the hunger!

« »

A felt need is the writer's cue. A need is already proved to be a human need by the fact that he *feels* it, and this is also proof of its interest, even though *he* alone, for all he knows, feels it. The need may be at first scarcely conscious in him but so long as he feels it, he can work in fair faith that sooner or later it will become recognizable, if not definitely by some simple designation (such as, say, "revenge") then by the form or pattern or plot or tone or texture, etc., that his poem or story takes as he works on it.

No matter what the need, or "hunger," may be (shameful, bitter, preposterous, delightful, reasonable, exalting, normal, abnormal, and so on forever), come in on it. That is, come in to the performance. At least enter seriously enough to restore your sense of what that thing "interest" really is, if you feel you have lost it. If pornography cues you to find again such elusive but ever existent hungers as, say, those for a particular tender insight or for the freshening effect of a child's trust, go ahead. This does not commit you to pornography as an objective—or to sentimentalism or rhapsodic religiousness or barbaric violence. It is only an activation of the *feeling* of interest.

« »

The need for food or love or vindication or fame, or for any ever-evident things and non-things, too often requires no rediscovery. These needs are the regular, standard interest-cues for the hack writer. His main effort is to reduce any subtlety these thematic needs may seem to have, so as to match the small amount of subtlety in the minds of his kind of readers.

The stories by the paltry writers are usually on about the same plane as the juvenile story of the lad who wants a bicycle or the lass who wants a horse for his or her "very own" and "more than anything else in the whole world," and who then does some commendable deed to acquire it. In the "adult" version the bike may be a wife, the horse "all this and Heaven too," but the acquisitive motivation in either version almost goes shallow, like a mercantile theme. The gimmie gimmick elicits a kind of interest that passes away into nothing after it has been gratified, because the objects of the quest, though they may at first have on them the glamor projected from some warmly glowing inner desire, are (and continue to be) unsignifying externals. In "achieving" them, the heroes do not change, nor does their "conquest" make any significant changes. Suppose they fail; there would be no significant changes either.

The quest for the Holy Grail may seem to be a type of story whose motivating hunger is toward the theme of acquisition, but in any version you may essay of the story, you will have to deal with inner as well as outer significances, whether the seeker succeeds or fails. His triumph will have tragical overtones, his failure the overtones of a continuing faith. Our hungers, profane or benign, are vital or else are only whims for trash.

« »

Interest is a given and accepted promise of meaning. A poem cannot keep this promise if a reader is unwilling to take a promise. A poet should not trouble about readers who do not trust him.

« »

The trick by which you snatch at a reader's attention may in the next moment destroy his confidence. It's one gambit to elicit his skepticism and then change that into curiosity. It's another gambit, and a detestably bad one, to bring forth his doubt so that you can challenge it with a mystification that's higher browed than it is. *You* may awe him but your *story* will lose him.

A writer can never make amends for a failure of imagination in himself by saying the kind of thing, or in such a way, that will cause the reader to feel it's his own failing.

« »

Readers are more disposed to be unfair to poems than poets are to reading. Sometimes, if a poem interests a reader who later dismisses it because he "can make nothing of it," *he* does the dismissing.

Perhaps the poet too felt he could not make anything of it; he had to produce it nevertheless. He had to bring it to a state in which he could read it. (Or merely say it.) Most good poems were much more difficult for their writers to understand than, later, for their readers. Sometimes such poems continue to be more difficult for the writers, and the readers are the discoverers of the fuller significations. But in any case, a poet stays with the production of the poem because of its interest.

That is, he keeps holding it to its promise. Although he may not always know what signification is going to evolve, he keeps on knowing the poem more and more as an organism.

He feels undeniable intimations that the poem contains substance, frustrated as he may be in his striving to demonstrate it.

As a reader of anyone else's poem, he knows that it cannot be justly denounced as "inaccessible" as long as it engages his interest. No person can be fairly judged as unfriendly whose face asks that we look into it.

Far from protesting that poets should try to know what it is to be a reader, the readers should try to know *how* it is to be a poet.

« »

Interest is not ease. It is complicity. This is not always comfortable.

To be interested is to be between our present condition and a new one that is not yet ours.

Interest is not submission. When you bid for a reader's interest you are not requiring supinity but alert participation. (A work continues to be a work after it is finished. That is its "life.")

« »

Most poems today, and even the finest in accomplishment, and most paintings, likewise admirable, hold little more than momentary interest for us. It is because they do not live with us. They do not because their makers were not really interested in them, had no deep, engrossed, wholly committed passion for the *subject*.

If the subject is but incidental to the act of writing a story, the story will lack the passion that warms the flow of interest, no matter how passionately devoted the author might be to Literature, or to the Short Story as a literary type, or to the career of authorship.

Such a poem or story sits in a show window, the sterile light casting a gloss over it. This is pseudo-interest. As we read it, the prevailing impression is one of non-necessity.

« »

Reviewers like to commend writers for the absence of self-pity or to rebuke tham for its evidence. Pity itself, at various times and in various societies is taboo. There is a lot of fumbling psychologizing that to *feel* pity is bound to be pathological and to have it is to be unavoidably contemptuous. This is the kind of rationalism a genuine poet sees through as silly obtuseness. There is a world of difference between showing pity (or respect, or devotion, or patriotism, or chastity) and having it; and in an ostentatious society the showy kind of pity is the only kind known to exist. A poet or fictioner, though, who does not feel some pity for himself, likewise will not feel the self-pity going on in somebody else, and this perversity subsequently forbids him to feel any other kind of pity. This amounts to a major deficit in feeling. It is a sure prevention of interest.

Let us ask ourselves, "Have I forgotten how to weep? Haven't I anything to cry about?" We would probably discover we have a good deal of weeping to do, if we did not shirk it—if we were not trying so superstitiously to be completely sane, "adult," "adjusted," comfortable, no discomfort to anybody else.

Among us there are writers who have sense enough to scorn such euphemisms as "passed away" and yet who are making quasi-stoical euphemisms of themselves. And of their styles.

Poetry and fiction as arts rose out of a cultural temper in which there was no anaesthesia, in which the art of tragedy was the essential hygiene. It was, instead of a prescriptive avoidance of pain, a prescriptive mode of withstanding it.

In having to withstand the undeniable actualness of our mortality—of downright death, the chalk-white aliens our dear bodies become—we hunger to know what to do with it in our minds. And because we can never gratify that hunger and can never withstand the grief of the pain by shutting off our feelings, our emotions and intellects, they combine into that mood which is so inadequately designated by the term "interest."

No philosophical or creedal anti-materialism, no abrogation of the human senses can do away with this process of poetic and dramatic interest and produce another effective one in its stead. If you cannot feel fear, if you cannot have pity—or if you *will* not—there is no vocation for you in poetry or fiction as essential arts.

## III

Violence is always an interest-catcher, yes, and that is why so many fictioners, even the avowedly literary ones, make much use of it. Life is violent. That is their justification. But this justification does not suffice for a work of art if the interest in the violence springs out of the complacency that "this actually happens without happening to me." That is interest repudiated. The repudiation continues; the work of art does not.

Such disengagement is evasion—in any of the arts. It is *an*aesthetic distance. Nobody can be aesthetically interested without having his humanity involved. The intellectual beauty of a "pure form" is that it is *our* performance.

« »

Cruelty can be an interesting *subject* honestly, on our part, but not other than dishonestly a *contrivance*.

A subject for a poet or novelist includes this or that as a theme, or several themes, but always because the writer sees the thematic possibility and develops it; likewise "slant," or "angle," and "point." But much more than that, a subject for an imaginative production amounts to what Quakers call a "concern." If we insist upon being so "objective" that we will not consider imperatives from within ourselves as germane, there are the imperatives of the object (i.e., the scene, the animal, the eventuation, and so on) with its apparent actualities and its latencies for us to consider. Our acceptance of the necessity of doing so, and our diligence in doing it, will contribute to what as writers we may understand to be a concern. This may be as unemotional as the mood demanded by a mathematical structure or as shocked a feeling as is caused by the killing of a child; and yet in either extreme of idea, the writer's response is an imperative responsibility which puts him to task. As soon as a writer understands what a subject is as an intrinsical concernment he need not resort to manneristic contortions to avoid either ultra-intellectualism or any sentimentalism.

He knows his charge.

## IV

Regardless of how cogent a philosophy a writer may use in his program of anti-art, anti-literature, anti-drama, and so on he cannot make his fiction interesting if he keeps repeating the story of human reduction. The formula which goes, someone-is-anybody-is-nobody-is-either-an-object-or-nought, may at first have the impact of dire news to smug minds, but it annuls interest as a factor in fiction.

« »

Despite the present pandemic dismay over the vanished concept of personal selfhood, each of us is still here with his consciousness. And in it our imagination demands fiction with characters that are persons who individually are at least identifiable enough to us as readers, if not to themselves as beings, so that we can see *who* as a *who* and not as a *what* in the story. As a mere *what*, no character is any longer of fictional interest however much of a specimen he might be for science. Personhood is indispensable to fiction.

« »

Having a subject that is a concern, in order that your story will be thoroughly interesting, is not a lightly effectible requirement. A concern is feckless unless there is passion in it.

The resort to an ersatz subject, and especially personal identity as such, is a most present danger. It is that the writer, along with his contemporaries, is punch-drunk and almost passionless. He tells himself he is seeking his identity when in reality what is lost is his power to *feel*.

For want of a subject by which he might identify his story as a story, he has his characters lack a sense of their identities.

He may contrive the stories in such a way that he can say the situations, incidents, characterizations, and the angles of narration are all symbolical of the doings and anguishes in the search for self-identity. The characters must fail in the search of their identities because the author no more knows what those identities might possibly be than he knows what to have for a subject.

Moreover, personal identity, far from being a *subject* for a story or poem, is a factor in the process of creating one, and also in that of witnessing such creation. It, to a productive mind, is not a thing or entity or state that you can lose or find; it is an activity, in the same sense as living is.

« »

Whatever a person does consciously makes him more conscious of his own actuality, and the more aware he is of himself as a conscious being the more aware he can be of other selfhoods than his own. And the more profitably so. The profit is knowledge, a further knowing. By knowing himself as a knower and by distinguishing one knowing from another knowing, he also distinguishes this knower from that one. That is, he knows which one he is. Which one he is now. But also which one he was then, and consequently which one he might possibly be sooner or later. It is an activity of the mind, a minding of oneself, a "selving" of the mind. A process.

Identity is a process of being, self-identity a process of self-being, and self-being a process of kenning other beings.

« »

A character is "lifelike" and an action is "real" because he is interesting.

He can be a phantasy and if interesting enter into our existence as a participant.

Lifelikeness in good fiction is more than similarity. It is more than simile-making. The good feat in fiction-writing is a symbolical identifying. The author says, life and living persons are this, and the reader's mind replies with the converse. *If he is interested.* Fiction is metaphor. A good fictioner, like a good poet, makes a verb of "metaphor"; he metaphors much of what he puts his mind to.

## V

After one who is rich in talent has learned to write a story, why does he nevertheless fail in interest? His materials, approach, tactics, attitude, and so on all seem interesting enough but never his story taken as a whole.

The trouble often is that we forget that it should continue to interest a reader long after he has finished it. But how? The "slow burn" is good but there is more to an abiding "afterinterest" than that.

Being a participant, or a witness, or a reader does not except rarely satisfy us as knowing how to feel about something that has happened. One hungers acutely to know what to do with it in one's own mind. That is what the Greek tragedies accomplished for people, who already knew the story of each.

That is what a story must still do for a reader today if it is to be anything but a mere record or chronicle or report, if it is to be fiction, which means taking mental—yes, psychic—possession of a happening, re-realizing it.

In the case of a story or a play, the reader makes this acknowledgment tacitly, not completing it until perhaps a very long time afterward, but as the narrative is drawing to its close, he is already beginning to feel the process of doing something with it in his own mind, and its continuation afterward becomes a more and more satisfying engagement.

There is no technique for writing a story in such a way as to make it do this to a reader. For it is what a story is in the first place; it is a conceiving. You conceive a story as being a satisfying, or even gratifying, mental handling of what happened. A special "doing something with it" in your mind. And you keep on seeking this satisfaction all the way through the writing. It is as if this "doing" of yours were a perceptible motion to which the reader's mind responds kinaesthetically. This part of writing fiction is as much knowing how to live while you are writing a story as it is knowing how to plan and execute it.

« »

People argue back and forth over Art vs. Content, over whether what-is-done is more important than how-it's-done. Here is the hardworking writer's working answer.

Somebody urgently suggests a subject, and the writer fends with "I wouldn't be interested in reading this if somebody else wrote about it—" and he stops midbreath, for he was about to add "no matter how well."

He halts himself because he knows in his guts that if he ever ceases to be interested in *how well*, he will cease to be a writer.

"How well do I think I could do this?" Part of him may say, "Not very well" and part of him will whisper that he *feels* a possibility. So there's some suspense in the very story of this work's coming into being. Interest.

This dramatic tension is the only premonition *any* writer, however great a genius, can have of a work in progress as to its consummate merit. It is an early phase of what is a good writer's ultimate hope: that he will have written better than he knows.

« »

It is better to hold to your mood than to your theme. It is better to know ahead just what spell you wish to make than what point. It is safer too. If we take a poem as an example this precept is too evident to writers to require discussion, but not so a story.

A story which fails because it seems pointless or themeless but which nonetheless produces a tenacious spell will not be so flat a failure as the one with a definite theme and neatly made point if that story neither has nor produces a mood.

Scientists and didacticians put forth their facts and tenets and inferences for as moodless as possible a perception. They elicit an interest that has been formed *before* they make their presentations. The fictioner is grateful for such already existent interest even if it is cold, but he does not count on it. However favorable it may seem he must replace it with another—go it one better.

« »

Prophets and preachers reprove mankind for having the experience but missing the meaning. If that is missed the experience too fades into oblivion. A poet can re-utter a meaning in such a way that he restores the experience. Then both are for mankind to have and keep.

There is a way, though, of providing or re-instancing an experience through poetry and fiction so that the meaning clings to it and the reader gets it more or less consciously. He can't miss it without missing much of the experience at the same time. His getting both at the same time at the first or second reading, with perhaps more impingement of the experience than of the meaning on his mind—this getting is interest at its best. The author accomplishes this, to a large extent, through his alert use of connotations.

The thousands of ambitious writers of fiction who assiduously learn the techniques and who perhaps have a hoard of good materials, yet fail to turn out any but inert narration, usually are oblivious of connotation as a magical factor. There are cases of hundred-thousand-word novels being written, without the author once being aware of a connotative actuality or the lack of it.

Connotations do more than add interest; they breed it. Watch for them with the many eyes of your mind, with your memory awake. Beware of untoward and miscuing connotations. There are plenty of propitious ones waiting to come in, close kin to your theme, so long as they're welcome.

# Plotting

## I

You are in trouble the moment you ask about your material, or about an "idea": How can I get a story out of it?

The fiction writer's genuine artifice is not a trick of forcing a proxy story out of something in which there is no inherent story; rather he has a knack or an eye for discerning in some material or situation the *dynamic* of a story.

This dynamic is not a mysterious thing even if it is often not easily discerned. It is the eventuality suggested by the material (the scene, person, circumstance, and so on). That is, events, rather than *solely* a mood or an impression or an amazement or a moral, strike you and invite speculation.

The more inherent these events are as they seem to ensue from the matter the more likely they are to plot themselves into a workable design.

« »

Many an excellent story is thought out before it is written, but it is the story and not the mere plot, the complex living entity and not the abstract structure, that figures in this thinking. In its embryonic stages, the story's skeleton grows along with its entire body.

No stage or part should be regarded as a separate thing. Every bit of it, from the "germ" to the total forming up of its significance, should be a living contiguity. Always think of it as an organism.

« »

## *Plotting*

A good plot is more than a nicely timed schedule of occurrences and correlative action. It is more than a kinematic pattern. It is an evolving system too complex to be reduced to a single scheme of events, or a neat plan. For it includes many provisions that in a superficial notice do not appear implicated in the movement, or growth, of the plot. Their *effect* is all that the reader need receive, and the less aware he is of them the less impeded the effect; but the author's awareness of them stimulates his inventive abilities.

« »

A good fiction-writer is quick in seeing and letting his plots evolve. Like a poet who has cultivated his sense of symbolical possibilities, the fictioner develops his sense of eventualities (which are also symbolically potent). He feels that his story is good because somehow it has always been a story. Herein, perhaps, is the reason why the more tricky some writers are at plot-making, the more paltry their stories prove to be.

« »

A plot is most likely to make itself, *evolve,* when you become interested in events for their propagativeness. One event produces another. This can go wild, get nowhere. But such danger is no worse than that of inattention to the potentiality of each event you deal with.

« »

If you plot the way you would pack a trunk, the episodes will jam-fit into the story neatly but the events in them will not *happen*. Any plot action has to do more for the story than just fit in.

« »

Many a fictioner, upon looking through a story of his, perhaps one he wrote years before, is surprised to see in the plotting certain merits he had never noted either in the writing or in the first after-readings. Congruencies, counterpointings, niceties of sequence, symbolical turns, rhythmical occurrences, and many other felicities emerge for the first time. He may realize that if he had consciously striven for these effects when he composed the story the straining would have appeared and there would have been preciousness in them.

« »

There are many auxiliary plot-properties; only the author can know how many there may be for his story, and just what they are.

Sometimes these are so numerous that the ordinarily evident plot itself seems reduced in their midst, and then reviewers speak of a "plotless" story, in which "nothing happens and yet everything happens." The readers confess they are unable to say just what it is that holds and impresses them.

## II

Though a fictioner must "make up" and select and arrange the events, he does not try to cover up or camouflage this process; it dissolves into its effects. Much of the intelligence here consists in his first regarding certain events as probable.

All this time he has an eye for the *necessity* of the relation between the events. With all of his inventive mind allowed free play, he deftly (and often with pangs) disregards his importuning chance fancies and his meddlesome extraneous pet ideas. (Extremely difficult.) For the incidental whim weakens an otherwise sound narration and makes it whimsy. And it is precisely that menace the intelligent reader dreads. He does not like to submit his mind longer than an instant to the whims of another. But to another's *design*—to an organic significance—yes.

« »

In life our control of events is much more limited than in our writing of fiction, where we seek to maintain control throughout. Life, however much we may program it, continues to be a mystery, and much of this is the mystery of the future. In fiction, it takes an amount of plotting just to keep the future mysterious. In life, anticipation of events spices them for us; in fiction it is more likely to spoil them.

Although fiction is usually a past-tense business, it is largely an art of handling futurity.

« »

Many writers who cannot invent a plot or even conceive a story-idea go in for historical and biographical fiction because the plot seems to be ready-made. But they often find out in the course of the work that the plot is hardly half-made. A chronological scheme for the plot is full of stumbles, discontinuities, pseudo-themes, misemphases, sags and snags. So fiction-making, *i.e.* artifice, comes into requisition.

« »

As you write one incident after another, feel them accrue as signifying events. As you complete the story, ask yourself, Wherein does the total eventuation in the narrative coalesce? You nor your reader may be able to point this out sharply; that is, with one finger, but maybe with three or four. If so, the events most likely attain to that gratification which is rightly called *story*.

« »

After reading a satisfactory story and reflecting upon the concatenation of the events in it, we may note that these had been "programed"—that some of the slightest incidents that had at first seemed to occur as fortuities conjoin to form a significance. So, if we hanker after hints of purposiveness in existence, we shall respect the story for its teleological earnestness.

Inasmuch as its artifices seem then to be matters dictated by destiny, they will not seem to be artifices but rather to be the integral content of the story.

Because the coincidings mean something, they seem to be more than *mere* coincidences. Because the author has each thing that happens a consequence of prior happenings, meaning seems inevitable. No coincidence occurs merely to solve a technical problem for the author: *e.g.*, to relieve suspense built up beyond the inherent resources of the story, or to turn a crisis by resorting to a meaningless accident that deprives the crisis of meaning.

« »

To avoid meticulously all coincidence is as bad for fiction-writing as to make heedless use of it.

We must distinguish between the discrete, bare-fact coincidence, whose only credential is that it is possible, and the rooted coincidence.

The rooted coincidence is a result of probables which are already there in the story or which a narrator is reasonably certain would be in the back of his readers' minds, perhaps more readily available to them by way of his having carefully used the indirect device of suggestive details.

« »

A coincidence can be valid, and what makes it valid is that it functions signifyingly. When a fiction writer understands this, he is close to the soul of the art. But he cannot understand this unless he understands it the other way around also: that a symbol functions because it is itself a coincidence; it is often a complex of several coincidences.

« »

In life we are struck by a coincidence if it resembles artifice; in art we dislike any artifice, especially a coincidence, unless it has some significance that is latent in life and that life itself does not formulate for us. Life produces coincidences but it takes art to produce dynamic symbols.

A symbol is an embodiment of coincidences, a storage battery of signifying energies.

« »

The usual reason why a coincidence strikes a false note in fiction is that it may be transparent as a mechanically contrived design. And yet what is a story if not a design?

« »

Design is not easy to achieve as art. Nor will our minds let us continually avoid design, order, pattern, rhythm, coincidence. We cannot behave or think wholly at random. A machine can be set so that it will give numbers at random, never making a discernible pattern, although the machine is itself a mechanistic pattern, but if *we* try to give out numbers at random we fail, because our minds, which are non-mechanical, will eventually name numbers so that they occur in a pattern.

Art is unpreventably order. Difficult as art can be, it is not impossible. Easy as the neglect of art might be, we cannot possibly keep art from beginning.

« »

The story-maker who resorts to coincidences to effect a *coup de théâtre*, or who employs the *deus ex machina* with them, is outside of our considerations here, because he works in bad faith, *except* when he is writing wacky farce, satirical whimsy, or any comedy in which the accidental breaks up patterns in order to suggest some forgotten but valid design, or hint the need for a new one that is valid. In these exceptional instances there is good faith because there is a tacit understanding between the writer and the reader that they can play as if they were naïve since they know they are not: a case of "when you call me that, smile."

The ancient story-maker who used these devices backed himself and his audience with the good faith of their belief in fate, destiny, the unpredictably assertive gods. In the trashy suspense stories contrived by modern writers who use surprising coincidences to extricate a character (and the author) from a difficulty, or to strike a sensational effect, the bad faith is the exploitation of a presumed naïvety in the reader—especially in juvenile fiction. Or else the author is himself too crudely naïve, and too empty of philosophy. He is artful but inept. When we examine the nature of coincidence as a *symbolizing process*, let us not confuse ourselves by thinking of such writers.

« »

An event as it occurs is action, somewhat as a motion is concrete to the ken of a deer, which may not note an object until it moves. A symbol is like such a motion; it is as attractive to us as it is concrete to begin with. And it is as valuable to us as it yields significance to go on with. It is especially valuable if the significance would be beyond the ordinary reach of our minds but for the suggestive power of the concreteness: if the symbolizing activity memorializes feelings we had not yet quite phrased, or if it brings out ideas we scarcely knew we had.

« »

If you are writing a history or a biography, include as many coincidences as you can be certain of as facts. The tacit understanding you have with your reader that you are reporting and not fabricating the narrative will imbue each coincidence with excitement for his imagination. The fact that is unlike fact excites the imagination the more for being a fact.

In history—impersonal or personal—factuality is the ever necessary basis, but if the writer has all he can do just to supply this basis, he is likely to be boresome. If he has any skill he will arrange the facts so that there will be surprises. Coincidences in events are ready-made surprises.

If you are writing fiction, factuality is not the basis, however much you intend to use the realistic or the naturalistic techniques. The basis is the experienceableness of what you set down, and of it *as* it is set down. Your use or avoidance of coincidence in events depends upon what it will do for or against the experiencing.

You have a tacit contract with your reader: Lend me your imagination and I give you my promise to respect your intelligence. Reason with me for a while and you will *feel* this thing I am telling you.

« »

Myth is a reasoning *toward* coincidence (not *from* it). Its authority is the imagination.

Imagination reasons confidently in the form of myth, because the probability of coincidence is greater than sluggish minds are wont to believe. The active writer therefore should have an affable expectation of coincidence and myth as processes within himself. Both are either spontaneous or sternly deliberate steers toward truth.

« »

Consider the myth-making tendency or necessity in the plotting of historical or biographical fiction. Factuality prefigures essentially in both kinds of narrative. When the writer has at hand all the facts he can find or can make use of, he must present them as a story. They become more than a citation "for the record": they become the enjoyment of a belief. Whether this is lasting or only tentative, it is worthwhile.

« »

Dialog makes the factual story much more experienceable than it could be otherwise. The most extensive research is unlikely to turn up enough of the right kind of conversation. And yet you do not wish to be arbitrarily fabricative; you do not wish to subject the unfictive characters to your hit-or-miss whims any more than you do to force them into your fixed preconceptions. At those opportune points where dialog is called for, the author asks himself, "Given all this data, and visualizing with it as vividly as I can, what can I imagine as most likely to have been said?" *All* fiction, really, is based on such theorizing. It tries to historify itself. And what is this practice, in either case, if not the use of circumstantial evidence, which is the kind we use in most of our reasonings.

## III

If we hope to write a story rich in its aftereffects, the likelihood is that we have a treasury of details about what happened before the story opens, about the underlying situation, and about this and that character's disposition. We can more or less plausibly or awkwardly set these matters forth as introductory facts, the author candidly accommodating the reader.

But such is seldom the actual effect. When we make it easy for ourselves by doing it simply and, as we suppose, "naturally," the chances are that we'll retard the movement so much that the matters will no longer seem to be an integral part of the story. Or only collateral to it in a loose, even sloppy, way. The exposition becomes one distinct element, and the plot another distinct element. This used to be no embarrassment, but the art of fiction has developed a lot.

The alternative is not at all easy, ever. But it can be truly natural. It is to regard exposition as a *function* of your plotting, rather than as an accessory to it.

« »

The only place for direct exposition, authorial analysis, or expository anecdotes is at a point where the problem-as-an-issue has been placed *through narration* (that is, through the progress of the plot) squarely in the reader's hold. If he wishes to examine it more closely, perhaps brooding over it, he will be grateful for whatever will assist or intensify this mental pleasure. Not until he holds the matter in his own arms, feels the heft of it, can he feel that he's asking for it, and that you're not loading it on gratuitously.

« »

As the plot develops, more and more is impending, and the reader senses in each rightly pitched detail as he comes to it an increasing imminency. This is more than the tension of suspense: it is also an intensification of the importance of each detail you supply.

« »

We cancel the character of whatever is complex in its nature when we attempt to make it simple—to reduce it to a few aspects. But we may well show only one or two of the aspects at a time to catch the interest of a reader who would soon fatigue upon sight of the full complexity. This piecemeal interest may be meager in comparison with the richness that we may reserve for him and that he can accept a little at a time.

The skill a writer has in making such seeming "simplification" is as good as his ability to hint the reserve. This is narrative skill, for a story is a complexity. This narrative skill works with similar profit in a complicated exposition, e.g., a treatise.

« »

Cutbacks should have a plan. In a haphazard occurrence, they will seem to importune the narrative, and instead of *advancing* it, they'll interrupt it, and undermine the buildup of the interest.

This plan is a kind of secret subplot of your own. The reader will not at first be aware of it, and yet he will be responsive to it. This would be because the cutbacks occur in a kind of rhythm. Once this rhythm is established, as it will be with, say, three cutbacks, you can vary it strategically. By then you have established an expectation of the next cutback, and it can come a bit sooner or later than expected, according to some advantage you may see in doing either.

« »

The *place* where any item of information is given in a deftly worked short story or novel is as vital to the dramatic enhancement as the *way* in which it is given. And therein may lurk some guile on the part of the overly astute author.

In all good faith between author and reader, there must be recognized certain moments at which particular facts would surely emerge because the action or the characters would really come out with it. Only the tyranny of the author would prevent it.

This arbitrariness has been practiced by some esteemed writers, and some of their admirers have studied it under the rubric of the "art of withheld information." This is probably because of the game in it: the admiration for smooth sleight of hand, at best a kind of entertainment, a *diversion*, in the double sense of that word. Or else, when it occurs in decidedly serious fiction, it can be taken as a mocking of the way in which humanity is arbitrarily pushed around by unrecognizable forces. But an author is recognizable as such even when he is anonymous.

It doesn't comport with the art of fiction to use poker-player's tricks on a reader. Besides, it's a kind of unfairness that presupposes a most unlikely naïveness in fiction-readers.

All the more regrettable is it when a gifted writer resorts to such dodges in his plotting. A vitiation sets in at the place within him where his prowess in fictional ingenuity originates.

## IV

There is no telling all the accessories a writer might find for that very organic kind of plot that is a buildup of power in feeling. Or a structure of feelings. Connotation, though, for this purpose deserves a good deal of our attention.

If connotation matters greatly in a poem, there is no good reason why it should not do likewise in a story. Especially in the plotwork. There is a difference, though: the connotations as they occur in a poem may be such that as we read it we are likely to increase rather than impair their effectuality by being focussingly conscious of them. They might not be immediately effectual, and a studious reader might activate them, and that too could enhance the enjoyment of the poem. Only if a reader studiously isolates each and every connotation taxonomically will he "kill" the poem. (Still it is amazing how some poetry survives vivisection.) But in the plotwork of a story, the connotations have their best effectuality when the reader is not specifically conscious of them, when he simply responds to their subtle nudges, as part of his submission to the current of the tale.

This is so for the author too as he writes through the story for *the first time*. He lets the connotations come or not come into the wording and instancing as they chance to. *Afterward*, though, when he reads and rereads his story to shape it for maximum force and best feel, he will be wise to ferret out and scrutinize every possible connotation and come up with some emending ones where needed.

The criteria here are whether the connotations further the plot, sensitize the reader for the impacts of it ahead, deepen the course it is taking, help to fuse it with the signification that is in the embodiment of the story, and so on. Do not be afraid to have this seraphic shrewdness.

« »

It is not only our choice of words, our descriptive touches, our sharply heard and espied details that are profitably connotative in fiction-writing; it's the actions too: incidents, events, episodes.

Unless a fictioner is as investing as a poet in the potency of connotation, the result will tend to be thin, forgettable narration.

« »

The dynamics of fiction glow by virtue of their connotations if these are congruent. So long as they are, the more of them the better; so long as they belong, none of them can occur if it would crowd the others. (The process of accordance takes care of that; only if there are conflicting connotations will there be a jam. The accordant ones may overlap, but not overtake.) The chance efficacy or chance infelicity in their occurrence need not worry us if we are aware enough of enough of the favoring ones. They are likely to breed still other favoring ones that we shall not be aware of but that will affect the reader, too, subconsciously. Then the unfavoring ones, which are as likely to occur as weeds are in any garden, will be of but feeble effect. (The more fertile your soil the fewer the weeds in your lawn.)

« »

Whether or not we intend to expose our utterances to the connotations that occur at random in other minds, various associative activities are inevitable in them, favoring or disfavoring the tenor of our story. Where we might intend a single hitching, a reader will hook on with a cluster of implications.

Perhaps this unpredictableness of connotation is the specific mystery of why some plays, styles of dress, forms of slang, and so forth (as well as books) are hits and some, often superior from a critical standpoint, are flops. The public, with its collective force of private connotations and of patent general connotation, is as much chagrined as the authors.

Even so, no other cast of mind has known and fore-known so many connotations as the writer's. One is tempted to argue that this was the aptitude which destined him to be a writer, and that writing is itself mostly a skill of commanding connotations in the affrays and truces of our speaking natures. If we have pondered well the peculiar ways of connotation as a rhetorical utensil we can be pretty sagacious about the specific effectuality of our connotations: whether general, or too much so and are stock, half-dead, or cultural (tribal, national, vocational), or personal but sharable, or private. Also, how a connotation may afford access to "levels" of meaning; how it may speed up or slow down a contemplation; how it may supplement any of the tropes. Despite the hit-or-miss precariousness of connotation, a good writer has perhaps a bit more control of it than the ancient ocean-faring navigators had of their voyages, with but few stars and no compass—and, think how very often they made port.

« »

In the plotwork of a story it is the *felt* connotations rather than the perceived ones that count. Particularly in inducing and augmenting suspense.

The several methodical strategems for contriving suspense can be deft and they may function with some subtlety. Yet this may be little else than a game played between author and reader: a systematized amusement consisting of honorable deceptions.

But *felt* connotations work differently. Though they are not deceptions they do sneak under to do their little stints in developing the suspense in a tale. The reader is not aware of them, yet he responds steadily to their suggestive power.

The felt connotation is what one feels when one sees in words a given idea, and feels that idea so immediately and surely that he does not, and need not, pause to ask himself the exact meaning of it. It is there tensing the suspense and at the same time increasing its implication. Thanks to the felt and cumulative connotations, the suspense-gathering plot becomes in its own sphere within the story what the symbolism of the whole story will be in the world at large.

At the end, that which is only felt and that which is definitely perceived as the "point" converge into an attained significance.

The suspense in such narration is a *telling* suspense.

# Letting a character live

## I

Characters happen. They happen just as events do. Characterization is a feat: knowing how to *let* characters happen.

In the great old myth even the original creator says to himself at least a dozen times, "Let there be . . ." and then it happens.

This letting is both easier and more complex than it seems. The ease comes from having already faced bravely the complexities instead of ignoring them. They are many, so many that there are more than enough to go around for each writer to have his own, and thus to give his characterizations his rare touch.

« »

No more can fictional characters be created directly out of nothing than could Adam, but must be formed from the dust of the ground and breathed into before they can happen to be.

« »

Nobody can tell you how to create characters. If you can create them you can't tell anybody else how to do it. It's a way of willing life to be, of letting it go on. A powerful willingness.

« »

We may love or hate some characters, or be indifferent to them (that is, maintain or pretend "objective detachment") but we must love and never hate them as characterizations.

The love we feel for our characterization is part of what makes a character "come alive." This is no less true with an odious character than with a likable one.

*Letting a character live*

If you must step back from your characters as though they had been eating onions, you had better rid yourself and your story of them. The novelist must handle odiousness, recognize it, impugn it; but he must also get close enough to it to see it. He must visit it. Get inside its house. (*Some*body has to do it from time to time; we cannot keep waiting for repeated comings of Christ.)

Like the author the reader too must let a character live. Some readers won't. They may hate the characterization because they hate the character. That is, as a person. So despite the validity of our characterization they will not allow it to be effective.

Effective characterization can be more dependent upon subjective factors within the reader than is any other element of fiction.

« »

As the effectiveness of a characterization is often unpredictable, we may feel some anxiety about one or another. In itself that's no danger signal. What we must not do is to let ourself become so anxious for effectiveness that we put most of our effort into it, for we'll tend to do so at the expense of validity, weakening and perhaps cheapening our characterizations.

A more confident way of working is to assume that a validity has its own effectiveness: can indeed suggest effectivities that are authentic, such as we otherwise might not have thought of. Looking deeper into our materials for a certain character, instead of into a bag of tricks for characterizing, sometimes results in the most plausible tactics.

« »

Instructors, editors, and reviewers often misjudge the requirement that characters be "lifelike," seem "real." Real and lifelike to whom? To fatigued minds having to deal with story after story as part of the day's work? To minds forever engaged in analyzing, typing, classifying everything and everybody? To stiff, literal minds? To minds embroiled in inner treacheries? To identity-seeking minds? . . . Or to minds receptive and resonant to connotation? Minds capable of enjoying the widening radiancy of a tone.

« »

We can have but little hope of making a reader see much actuality in our characters if he takes but unwilling, dim cognizance of his own actuality.

Especially that of his inner selfhood.

« »

The public is rife with literates who are attentive mostly to events outside their minds, to things rather than ideas. Whether naïve or loaded with the appurtenances of sophistication, they look for what costs them the least effort.

The habit of being retail customers pervades their "life style." These are the "consumer readers." They "buy" (believe) your fiction because you have done so much customer-service thinking for them. Every character must be plainly labeled, with all the ingredients named. If even then the customers are not sure just how they should feel about it, there are reviewers who will serve them as reliable inspectors and advisers.

« »

Not until a fictioner has freed himself from the obligation to please half-alive, unreflective readers can he feel his full power to inhabit his stories with animate characters. Once he feels this kind of liberation, he will write with a better confidence than he can have from adulation, alcohol, poses, or the satisfaction of having become instantly "honest" by insulting somebody.

## II

Look through a child's family of dolls and you will see that the one she is most devoted to is not necessarily the most "real looking." It is likely one which because of some quality in the little girl's vastly complex nature and untrammeled mind seems most to be her own baby.

Doubtless whoever made that doll (probably crudely whittled it out of a block of wood) tried with his craft to be providential, and we as critics of it may not think he did very well, but his work is functioning nonetheless. Why? Because of what he tried to anticipate: the child's psychic hunger *plus* the essential concomitant, her imagination. Thanks to that, *she* completes the process of characterization.

« »

The personification that takes place in the mind of a child with a doll is what we all let happen in our minds. We all have an animistic tendency. The geologist speaks of "stream piracy." The meteorologist uses girls' names for hurricanes so that the public can know "who" is which, and be interested and concerned and factually informed. The painter of a still life depends upon this animistic propensity when he makes characters of objects. They have "mood." They "live" although they can't move.

Things as people and persons as characters become viable because we don't want to be disappointed as to their existence so long as they're there for us to note: such disappointments entail doubts of our own existence.

« »

Through our growing out of infancy we learn how to characterize. (As authors *and* as readers.) This growth is from merely recognizing to *constructively* recognizing—somewhat as if in response to the question, "What do you make of it?"

As it is our nature to develop, development is the nature of fiction. Even when disintegration is the theme.

In the fiction writer's presentation of characters who are doing their living, the reality of them is not what the readers simply "see" or "find"; it's what they build into the characterization from their own inner realness—which is recognizable to them only as long as it too is developing.

« »

A critical moment in the reading of a story is the point at which the reader makes the scarcely conscious decision that he prefers to be uncritical of the possibility of the characters. That is, he becomes an engaged reader.

(This can occur at the very outset. Story makers have known this from way back. Just consider the highly effective ritual of "Once upon a time, there . . ." The conjuration here is mostly in the very first word, "Once," and the magic is in the focussing particularly of *onceness:* its immediate recognizability as a pointed-to happening.)

Our story, say, opens with items recognizable to our reader, and his mind says to the story, I'm started in my recognizing, so okay, go on. He feels his recognizing power increasing. An item, a glint of detail, a nuance, or a connotation forehints a new experience in recognition.

Once we have produced in our reader this confidence, our only worry need be that we won't spoil it. We won't if we realize that such confidence has its first existence within oneself, where it has been produced by dint of honesty and a combination of excitement and composure. By the time a reader's consciousness visits the writer's in the opening of a story, there's a blending of the two, so that a habitable sphere is present in which living beings seem not merely possible, but inevitable.

And inasmuch as our characters can only seem as real as the apparent realness of this sphere, our reader can have the anticipative feeling that those characters too are in masterly, dependable hands: that nobody in the story, for example, is going to be destroyed because of the ineptitude of the handling power. (The roughest, cruelest characters in a story full of violence require a sensitive, steady, providential hand of their author.) This ensurance at the very opening of the narrative is an intimation that the author's mastery is also one over his own personal vainglorious arbitrariness—his eagerness to seem superior, his whims of contempt, his grudges, his tantrums of spite.

Oh indeed he (that is, *we*) will have all these cursednesses. We must retain them for the widening range of the characterizations.

It's our confidently professional control of them, though, that contributes in great part the supportive tone and good carriage that readily take another mind right on into the story. And that helps a belief in the actuality of the characters.

« »

An engaged reader is a cumulatively recognizing one.

« »

An engaged reader is more conscious of himself simply as a being, a-being-here being, than he is as a reader.

Similarly, he is more aware of a character as a person than as a character. Even though a nondescript person! This is a fact you must rely upon. An engaged reader forgets he is reading. He is witnessing. "Witness my story" is what everything in us worth our right to write asks of a reader.

« »

In the conception of a character, and later in the reader's cognition, a potentiality within oneself emerges. Both author and reader take what was latent within them and render it into an overt "design" of a characterization, the author by way of invention, the reader by way of assent.

« »

A writer's self-exploration, when it is curious and game and tolerant, is in itself a labor of characterization. Good training for the novelist or dramatist, also good upkeep.

« »

What a reader is not blind to in himself he will not be unresponsive to in a character, however much the pang. Only those readers and writers who are not afraid to suffer in order to realize can be truly imaginative.

We can better project a characteristic for believability if we first imagine the experience of having it.

« »

The forth-and-back phenomenon of creating characters, in part, out of what's in ourselves, and they in turn increasing in us our narrative powers, can become a resonating force. Once such a resonance is started, all else moves along with it, even unto the reader. That's one reason why a weak personality in a story can have so strong a characterization that the reader finds it stirring.

« »

Never mind the perennial debate among writers and mentors: do characters make the story or does the story make the characters? You can have it both ways. Let the theorizers fight it out academically. Narrating is a different kind of struggle, a different kind of knowing, another kind of knowing what and how. You *must* have it both ways.

Regardless of whether it's evident in the finished composition, there is constantly going on between the elements of your work while you are doing it a good deal of reciprocating. If there isn't, you're working stiffly. And with cut-and-dried stuff. If it's alive with reciprocal activities, their complication and subtlety may almost drive you crazy, but you can well take heart that you may be bringing some characterful fiction into existence.

« »

Reciprocality is a dynamic that helps the writer conceive and produce characters.* It is also one that impels each character to function in his role. That is how characterization makes for story and story makes for characterization.

« »

In characterizations, as well as in the other elements of fiction, we must have a persistent curiosity about the effects of contraries. And also of mere othernesses. Not only conflicts but also conjunctions. And conjunctive conflicts.

When we make a conflict conjunctive we make a story. Also a characterization. Any two or more factors engaged in mutual modification.

Let's not argue about whether this is or isn't the long-honored principle of the "Imitation of Nature," or whether that's what a work of art should be. *Our* fact is that this is a process. And as such, what we say (say to ourselves if to nobody else) is that it *is* nature.

« »

In many characterizations there is a matching or a contrasting of special inner qualities between author and character.

These may be so conspicuous as to require some toning down. Or they may be latent, emerging only later, after author and character become used to each other. Also, these qualities may be either affinitive or antagonistic between these parties. Anyhow, there's interaction going on here; something is happening.

*"Conceive and produce" because these words specify what goes into the meaning of "create" a character. First, we need the *notion*, if but the merest notion, of one. And then we let and watch that notion grow and form, perhaps in many more ways than we'll use, but this growing and forming, even unto overpluses, is evidence of aliveness: the reciprocality is working for us.

Each of these qualities is an item of identity, author's and/or character's. Only piecemeal identities, but they'll serve.

« »

Identities that are no more than piecemeal within oneself can become entireties when viewed externally.

« »

A characteristic (or quality or trait) that may seem to us as possibly usable may be a matter entirely external to us. It may not be what we would call an instance of "piecemeal identity." Yet we may see value in it as the dominant note of a characterization.

Can we "do it cold"? Yes. And it will stay cold. If we do much of this cold work of characterization it will chill us numb.

We have to work warm just as we have to live warm. We have to do our not-me characterizations by letting ourself have some operative fervor.

We may strive to make a characterization as "objective" and ourselves as "detached" as all get out, but unless we warm up to the task itself the character won't be alive enough to be slapped down in a satire or to be regarded as even slightly impressive in a realistic story.

The process of characterization partakes of our inner heat. Perhaps none of this will seep into the *ostensible* character; some of it must go into the making of him. When we see this happening we have to admit that we can't utterly "objectify" anything alive.

« »

In a projected character the only traits from which we can rightly separate ourself entirely are those which we would regard as being universally alien, incomprehensible, or mysterious. The latter two of these anybody may simply *have*. The simple *having* of them by a character is experienceable in the imagination of a fictioner.

As for the odious traits, whether there is or isn't any chance of our understanding them, the having of them too is experienceable for us. No matter how we may despise anyone with those traits, no matter how much we'd wish to exterminate his kind, we still have to create him as a character if we want a story and not just a case report.

We have to produce his existence. The heat of our work impels our imagination in sharing his existence. We may be loth to put ourself in his place and we may be wise not to attempt to put our reader there, either. (In none of these "not-me" presentations is it assumed here that an introspective treatment or "subjective point-of-view" is being used.) During the contemplative phase of the work on a given characterization, however, a thoroughgoing fictioner must accept coexistence with each of his characters, ugly or beautiful, plain, colorful, shallow, deep, or what not.

« »

A good time to catch on to yourself as a not entirely guileless characterizer is when you're assiduous about eliminating yourself from the manifest process of narrating. While trying to keep your hand from showing in it you're liable to let your foot poke into it. Or what you intend as "detachment" may become a remoteness. By trying too hard to keep from showing your hand, you may cause your story to get out of hand. You may find you've lost touch with the characters.

## *Letting a character live*

« »

You can produce for yourself the semi-illusion that you're being "detached" from your characters; also for the reader the illusion that the characters are living in their own right without the least direct evidence of your being anywhere around, but you can't suppress the indirect evidence of your presence in the vicinity. Your choice of words, variations in emphasis; your way of varying the intensities and durations of focus; and many another skill special to you.

Thanks to your providence, your characters and their doings gain momentum, so that they seem to be going on their own. This is the only sense in which it can be said truly that "the story tells itself."

« »

We'd better not be content with even our most faithful realism. The best characterization, like the best acting, is something more than brilliant mimicry. It is a kind of reincarnation. Rather than repeating a life-type, it reproduces one that is a continuation of the same being, living now in a kindred realm, of theater or book: a world we ever make in place of the one we never made.

« »

A fiction writer's chief or only "inspiration" may be his great loathings. He may be capable of magnificence in certain hatreds, righteous or aesthetic. The objects may be individuals, types, or the human race. He may have admiring readers who share his detestations and are grateful for his wonderful slayings. (He may even have some admirers who feel little or nothing of his antipathy but who can enjoy the amazing spectacle of his bravura.) Inasmuch as he is truly a master, there may be no reason, moral or literary, why he should repudiate his forte and resign himself to the alternative which would be nonproduction. For he may be both a "moral force" and an artist. (Let's stay on the beam.)

Then what concerns us here is the possible, sometimes almost unavoidable, vitiation that such a writer must watch out for. He should beware most of two menaces to his art of characterization:

Self-exaltation, even when it would seem to be gained through a wide variety of brilliant despisals.

Slight, ever-lessening concern with probity.

His deterioration as a characterizer will set in as soon as he permits himself any continuation of these indulgences.

« »

In the art of abomination, we can't well hope to do characterization in depth and with more than a brief vitality unless we can sense in our species either some neglected potentiality or a lost strength, both of them benign. For, otherwise, a despicable figure in a story will cease to be really a character at all. We'll be merely extracting from our living models a lot of defunct examples, or severing a few fragmentary semblances, which can be used only for making effigies. The meanness, paltry frivolousness, and so forth of our depicted characters—even down to the merely incidental in-and-outers—require the authenticity of our roundly meditated conception of humankind. We must keep ourself reminded that our fingers can't be deft at picking up the little ones if our hands are too shaky to hold the big ones.

« »

No critic can judge solely by examining the description of a character just how vivid it would be in the mind of somebody reading the story, let's say, "intrinsically," and not for any ulterior, professional reason. Characters that are functioning reciprocally with the other elements of a story can be immeasurably connotative, and the array of connotations emanating from each visualized detail varies with the individual reader.

## III

Poor characterizations are often loaded with visualised details that stop instead of spur the imagination. The excessive load of notation (how aware we can become of the author's assiduity in notetaking!) blocks connotative activity.

« »

When you feel that somehow you've come to know more than your story permits you to show of a character, you can proceed with a surer hand. Don't, then, fret over not using all you have; never afterward regret it. It's always well to have that bit more left over.

« »

We can "design" the lives of our characters; that is, have discernible "pattern" there. But we must not importune them by throwing extra stuff in just because we want to show the stuff. (It's *their* extravagances the story is about, not ours.)

« »

A continual supply of visual details keeps a character constantly real before the eye of a reader. Not only that: it also vivifies the narration as a whole.

This is because, in the tissue of events constituting a story, any character is also a continuing event. He is that even if he does not act or change—even if you have to repeat his gestures and note the same facial markings in the many varyings of situation. Whenever he is cited as present, he isn't actually present if he's invisible. Nor if he is voiceless when he is supposedly saying something. He must *speak* and we must *hear* his voice, as plausibility is nine-tenths a sensory virtue.

Tissuing the characterization along with the eventuation is urgent, not solely for its strong effect upon readers; it's very much for the sake of your surer-handed feeling as you write.

An unpracticed or undeveloping fictioner will introduce a character with many concrete details, and never again actually "see" him or let the reader do so. Such a writer merely states the description; he doesn't *narrate* it.

## IV

Although we should have in the back of our minds the belief, and good evidence for it, that a character we are trying to present in the round is as complex as we ourselves are, he will have to be as a presence a simpler entity because of the mere time and space limits of reading and paper. These limits necessitate our very conscious control. So austere is this that to others it might seem to be achievable only through cold calculation. But we know also that the time-and-space factors which necessitate exclusions can and should occasion intensities.

By virtue of their *felt*—their experienced—apprehending, these intensities bring our imagination and our reader's into expansive activity.

« »

In the immediate world are persons as "fantastic," "inconsistent," "unrealized," "undeveloped," "pasteboard," "unlifelike" as any inept writer's defective characterizations. They have "written" themselves, or have let fortuity "write" them, as such. Each of us, in realizing his own essential identity is engaged in a labor of characterization. Much of a fictioner's art derives from this primary "practice." But the reason that some queer people make bad fiction of themselves is that they unduly "type" themselves; they make "characters" of themselves as desperate alternatives to jejunity. It isn't that they're content to accept their piecemeal identities as token entireties; they too miserably suspect themselves as abject nonentities. They're self-driven to falsity.

We can learn from their example better than from the examples to be found in inept writings just how *not* to do our characterizations. That is, we learn *we* must not contrive a fake so as to disguise a void. A character, though, may be doing exactly that and we write the story so as to bring out his self-betrayal.

People who in "typing" themselves as wholes at least take a trait that is there and may be unfair to themselves, but they are also in some small measure genuine. And perhaps clever to boot. Life, especially modern life, does not let us be in fact all that we are in potentiality. And so when we accept somebody's piecemeal identity as an entirety (although he may match only a particle of our selfhood, if any of it) we are living and characterizing as naturally and genuinely as he is. It's in pretending that where there's nothing there's something, or in substituting for something that's there something that's not there at all (usually because the existence of what's there is being denied) we go wrong. Nothing can be created out of nothing.

« »

The interactions between the elements of a story give impetus to the composition of it. That is, the interactions, with their connotations, favor the writer during his composition of the story.

And all this more or less happens again with the reader. If he feels the story's bid for his concern is valid the chances are that he will continue within himself the subtle, delicate process of satisfying depiction.

« »

A fact of life we must learn well is that if a writer is thoroughly honest with himself, he'll see that his vanity as a solipsist rather than his pride as an artist is what impels his ostentation.

"But I have to act according to *my* nature if I'm going to characterize people as *they* naturally are and as, I believe, only I can do it." Well, bravo to that—and also, tut! Any excess is good as a starter: what you do to get going is nobody else's business. But the going calls for control. The more the content and the force, the greater the need for control.

This control is what the literary theorizers mean when they say "objectification." It's an affair of holding the stuff of the characterization so as to integrate the character, so as to form *his* intrinsic selfhood, to let him have his own needs, to free him from our need for self-expression.

We then don't make an object of him, in the sense of object-as-a-thing, not that at all, but in the sense of somebody who is an ownself, however wretched or happy.

True, we often do get a character out of ourselves, originally, but the object and purpose of the characterization is to get him *out*, a good way out.

« »

It's not easy both to suggest and to define in our characterizing. How can we release a character to the reader's subjective contributory augmentations and yet safeguard what we see as the character's actual identity?

(To be sure, we can define the character tightly or neatly. But this won't always do; some characters *are* enigmatic and never will cease to be. We just have to let them. We must accept the fact that the art of characterization doesn't depend upon the avoidance of enigmas.)

What we have first to define against is *our* falsifications. They are usually personal prejudices, predispositions, peculiar likes and dislikes. If we don't like parsley, we should be able nevertheless to present a character who does, and to show his unpretended enjoyment of the flavor of it. If we confine our "sympathetic" characterizations to those diners who hate parsley and if we perforce make a point of having our disagreeable characters like it, we are falsifying.

Sooner or later this will become evident, one way or another, in the rest of our work.

As for the reader's falsifying biases, we can offset a good many of them by working for some complexity in characterization, resulting from the effects of one character upon another. Our control, part or complete, of this complexity induces the reader to forget his biases so as to receive the dramatic final impact.

## V

In characterization, control can become overcontrol. In getting away from arbitrariness we may manage our characters so highhandedly that this manipulation becomes only another arbitrariness, which some critics would seize as an opportunity to call our characters "puppets."

This stereotyped pejorative is really inapplicable. A fiction-writer, the truth is, might respectfully envy the puppeteer. And learn.

There's a good deal of character *creation* in the making of a puppet. It's a process that demonstrates how inimical to each other are creativeness and despotism. Like the writer, the puppeteer does his work with the hope of its turning out to be better than he knows. Even if different from what he had strictly expected. (Sculptors, puppeteers, fictioners tacitly accept the truth that what they desire to make lifelike must be allowed to have a life of its own.) As he puts the puppet into action, he feels its demands to behave in one way rather than another, a demand that gives the puppet the requisite individuality. And animation.

A puppet is fashioned with emphasis upon a dominant trait. This is similar to caricature, yes, but the moment he begins to act he transcends this as a limitation while retaining it as a characteristic. This is what amazes.

« »

You are more liable to over-manipulate and thereby falsify a character if you have him proxy for yourself in a story than if you proxy for him. In the former case you are probably either glorifying or vilifying in effigy. In the other case you're trying to feel what's in under the character's behavior and utterances, especially if you're using his point of view, and still more especially if you're presenting this introspectively.

It's the case of having him proxy for yourself, though, that needs some hard thinking about, because of one's dominant tendency toward autobiographical materials.

If one's true intent, say, is an out-and-out autobiographical novel, there's little danger of bad faith, even with the opportunity to make prevarication more plausible in the third person than in the first. In such a novel, the introspected (usually also the central) character often is a writer too. But when the introspected character is not a writer and when the author has him thinking and speaking like a writer, with a display of the author's wide resources for allusion, the characterization collapses.

No matter how much we may lust to show off how much we know, we should never force a non-writing character to do his private thinking as though he were a writer writing about somebody doing some private thinking.

« »

A very short story can have body if even but one character in it is a somebody and not a nobody. A ponderous novel can be bodiless if its personae lack bodiliness. Carefully descriptive stills or cinematizations of them aren't enough. They become *some*body in the story only as long as the story keeps on going and growing within them as you tell about them. That is, what's in them is also some of the story.

While you're telling who a character is and what he's like, you're telling the story too, just as much as when you're telling what's happening. Wherever this process stops, the story stops being a story.

« »

We body forth each character through eventuations that are constantly cumulative in effect. All the while we're describing him, however immobilized (in his casket, even), he's in the motion of the passage of time, a solidity or a wraith but not an abstraction, and no two successive moments are exactly the same; for this is story, perhaps not drama, but moving toward the dramatic.

« »

A writer may be a misanthropist and still turn out excellent characterizations. He may hate man angrily, yet write better portrayals than can those who almost go balmy in professing "love for all mankind." (Fiction that's the least bit serious holds man to account; it has a bit more sternness than clemency in its envisagements.) Nevertheless the bitterly rebukeful writer must retain respect for his art, and he cannot unless he has some for himself in his being an artist, which has its only possible existence in his own humanity.

What, then, is imaginatively respectable in *that*? What indeed unhateable? To ask this and to find and hold onto his answer is to provide authenticity for the way in which he views any character.

Man's vileness can be portrayed with dramatic truth because there is in our mind some conception of what is not vile.

« »

Among some fiction writers there's an inclination to make their characters inarticulate. As a symbolical hint of human inarticulateness in facing the vastitudes, or as a direct device for showing the helplessness of certain kinds of people in certain predicaments, this mode of characterization is advisable. It doesn't take much skill. It amounts to scarcely more than showing that a character is taciturn simply by not having him talk.

Some otherwise well-skilled writers, however, use this as a strategem: looking down on somebody can seem like seeing him "objectively." This may gratify a writer's hunger for illusions of his superiority, and his admiring readers will be grateful to him for providing them with the same kind of illusion.

He can get away with it. That's not the point. The point is, is it good faith? Can any writer afford bad faith? That is, within his private psychic economy?

## VI

One of the sorriest mistakes a fictioner can make is to take as a model of "Naturalistic" treatment of character the flattish things with human names which you find in stories purportedly written with "a cold, objective eye" or in the style of a "tough, hard-boiled" reporter.

The aim of such a fictional treatment may be to show the process of the *de*characterization of human beings in this age, but no process at all is there, let alone dramatized, if the figures in the story are already non-characters, and all that's to be narrated is the slight, vague transition into their becoming non-persons. Putting at the end a quasiphilosophical fillip about non-being doesn't help. A characterless story is a self-contradiction. A writer stymies himself permanently if he goes in for a reciprocality of annihilations. (Let it be repeated here: what *we're* concerned with is not primarily the harm being done to Literature, which has for a long time been too stout for its makers to worry about, but with our own impairment.)

« »

A character may be physically passive but he must be emotionally active to seem real. Even if he is a person in whom feeling and thought have died, he must be presented as *carrying* the dead weight of these if he is to be interesting as a person in the midst of life and not an insensible object with a human form.

If our story is about somebody who simply "goes dead on life," the going is the tale: how, in what special way he goes, or with just what wistful failure to be special. If there's no going, there's neither character nor story. As dead men tell no tales, dead characters let none be told.

« »

All good fiction, in being imaginatively rendered, is also imaginary. In our way of telling a story, we produce a spell or a mood or a state of mind or an illusion. Call it what you will, it's that within which a character can live, and without which he cannot live. We have many means for producing this spell: tone, rhythm, tempo, connotation, metaphor, word-sounds, colorings, and subtleties of our own that haven't names. They're imagination-quickeners. They're as indispensable for fiction as they are for poetry.

If we produce this spell we can make fairy folk, demons, exotics, and quixotics seem "real," animals "human," and objects "animate." If we can't produce that spell, our meticulously accurate "documentation" will not make even persons who are, or have been, alive elsewhere seem to be alive in our tale. They'll be figures of record but not characters who abide in our narration.

## VII

Care as much about how you are motivated in writing a story as you care about the motivations of the characters. But keep theirs and yours apart.

They may not, and usually cannot, know their real motives. You must know both theirs and your own. Theirs may become too complex for disentanglement, yours must tend toward that ultimate simplicity we call form.

The story must have its own fulfilment regardless of whether the characters have any or not, and yours can be none other than your story's.

« »

We'll do well to hold it as a private policy that *any* character, though he may have only a momentary presence in our stories, and though he may in no way resemble anyone that a reader ever saw or imagined, should have some validity for his function in the narrative. He may be the merest accessory—"just a prop," but he must be a human prop.

Then the readers apprehend the character as *consequential*, however slightly so. Even though they do not foreglimpse just what the fate of the character is going to be, they feel an imminence of consequences.

But we don't want any reader to respond with an unduly challenging expectancy; we don't want his mind to be halted by a niggling need to say, "So what?" We want him to feel there is in the offing some kind of whatness, so that he'll go on reading to find it.

This maintenance of a tension of overall consequentialness takes some doing on the part of the writer. It takes a combination of instinct and skill and abiding concern, aimed toward keeping the processes of unification active in the midst of turbulent complexities.

« »

Only when we are willing to view the problem of characterization *along with* (not just the same as!) the problem of living can we work as well as we'd like to. (The difference is that in art the most we can hope for is the *accompaniment* of it to "life"; neither can duplicate the other.)

People (not all of them) are concerned with who they are, and characters (not all of them) ditto. But the writer is chiefly concerned with the *actuality* of a character. Keeping that actuality. And never betraying it. Not for the plot. Not for the thesis.

## *Letting a character live*

When we invite a character to existence in our story we must respect both him and that existence as a composite actuality. If we switch this to something else, ulterior to that composite actuality, we'll ruin the characterization.

Literature past and present is stuffed with such ruination.

« »

No amount of vivid description, sensitive insight into an individual's feelings, or knowledge of human nature will produce the necessary illusion of a living person. It's because a character *does* something in a story that he does anything in a reader's mind, and so seems actually to exist. Vivid descriptions and perceptive analysis may add value to these doings but cannot substitute for them.

« »

Often, inhabitating your stories may be a character (or several such) who will have dimensions requiring the light of a reader's mind to be fully seen by him. Then you may wisely suggest what it wouldn't do to attempt to supply.

Have some faith, some working trust, in yourself as a reading-gauging writer. And in your reader as a writing-gauging reader.

There aren't, it's true, a great many of them. But neither are there of you. Fine characterization is a dedicatory job.

« »

The difference between a living characterization and a lifeless one, between animatedness and inadequacy, depth and flatness, is not altogether an affair of superbly chosen and worded details of visualization which trigger the imaginative reader's picture-forming processes. The character's predicament, his behavior in it, how it signifies to him and how it doesn't, what he realizes and doesn't and what he couldn't possibly realize, make him real to the reader who doesn't wish to be confined to readymade realizations but expects to carry on the task, which indeed is the very task of life, if there is any.

« »

A characterization may focus on an individual, or an "unindividual person," or on a group of persons or on a whole populace. In any case and in any event, the first or best or only reason you can well have for that focus is a certain unity. And the use of that unity to you is that it signifies; that is, it betokens more than what's immediately evident. (Just as each successive incident, or move of the plot, says, "There's still more.")

« »

A good writer should never allow himself to conclude that his expressiveness is limited to what he can find expressible. There's more to *him* than only this, and to what he has it in him to utter.

« »

A rose that's a rose that's a rose is a good solid image which we value for its selfness and its thereness, but that's all. For it is not a character, not even a "thing-character." A rose that's not more to us than a rose that's a rose is not enough of a one to be as much a rose as our imagination desires a rose to be. Our imagination is not content with an image solely but yearns for character.

« »

A characterization that is signifying in a story, rather than only plausibly and entertainingly instrumental to it, reminds the author and then the reader that no matter how simple and shallow and ordinary and even phony a living person might be, there's still in his experience of being alive a singleness. When we try to view this and to do so with some concern, we'll encounter a challenging mystery. This encounter happens with special force to us as writers because our very power to write originates in a mystery.

« »

A character signifies as a character, not necessarily by being presented allegorically or symbolically, but by being viewed as an intrinsicality. As such he is alone, whether he consciously feels so or not. If he is the least bit conscious of it, the truth of the commonplace observation "everybody down deep inside is lonely" becomes patent. But it's there in any case. And this is what the serious characterizer must be mindful of, even when he's portraying silly, shallow fools.

One's intrinsical existence is a mystery. It may not seem so to many persons outside of stories or in them; nonetheless we who write those stories must be aware of that "possible plus" in every individual characterization we attempt if we wish to impart to it a certain soundness, a certain authenticity. This may not be anything anybody can point out in the printed instance; it's rather in the "feel" of our work as we go at it. And in the "after-feel" of it that the reader gets.

« »

If you wish to write impressive fiction rather than grind out merely saleable stories, you'll not be content with intimating just the surface traits, except in the incidental or the light (i.e., "entertaining") characterizations.

The trouble with fiction (now that we have so much of it, so many different kinds, and such widely ranging experimentation) is not that there are too many unlifelike characterizations, but that too many are lifelike in too much the same way. Human beings are not so much alike as *beings*. If they were, the art of fiction would be as limited in scope and depth, almost, as an applied art is.

Doubtless, people do try to be alike in their fashions, mannerisms, mores, pretensions; and it's our job to show this. But often each such individual who imitates somebody else does do so in the belief that it's a newer or more acceptable way of being different from the people he doesn't like enough to be very noticeably identified with. There's a kind of pathos in this, worth a fictioner's scrutiny.

The writing kind of mind reads in such persons a palimpsest, seeing through the assumed overlays, which cannot be quite opaque to the undisdaining curiosity of the story-finder's eye. Even the dull, would-be duplicates when so observed disclose traces of singularity, perhaps a marooned wistfulness, a peculiar way of suffering from unconfessable impoverishments of selfhood.

« »

The discontent a reader voices in saying "There must be more to him than that" about a characterization has its origin in the seldom voiced but often felt idea: "There must be more to me than merely this."

*Letting a character live*

« »

People used to say of a town that it had so-or-so many "souls." This is the non-statistical, tersest, most uneuphemistic way of designating what we are. Each one of us is not just "people," which is hardly more than an abstract word.

Moreover, each of us feels he's a person and that he has at least a pittance of personality and that it's a compliment to be called a personage. But after he has been called that, he feels there's still more than that to an individual. We can call it "Element X" or simply "soul."

« »

Whatever it is, we feel that a soul is larger than the personality. No person who isn't a vain ninny wants to be reduced to his personality, even if he doesn't believe there's a ghost-or-spirit kind of non-thing that religious people believe in as their soul.

The soul-sized notion that each of us has of himself is a necessary egotism, the allowable minimum needed for self-respect. It's probably the meaning we have in mind when we speak of "human dignity."

« »

The well-developed fictioner, like a poet, is always working toward a transcendence.

# Dialog

If we regard dialog as *added* to the action of a story, it will be weakened, even though both the dialog and the action may in themselves seem strong. Dialog is not an interest-capturing device merely to accompany the action. Dialog is itself action. It is *the* action of a story no less than anything else that's going on.

If we think of it as the "spoken action," we'll know better when to use it so we'll feel the story gaining strength, and moving ahead, speech by speech.

The events too should be, in our minds, a kind of dialog. They occur, one as the result of another and also in reply to it. In *our* minds because it is almost exclusively a mental mode of working with the dynamics of the story. The reader simply receives the effect. Even if he is a keenly analytical critic as well as a wholehearted reader, he'll wish to enjoy the effect first, before he too goes to work on the story.

« »

We can stimulate inventiveness in fiction-writing by regarding the voiceless activities (incidents, and so on) as a collocution. Not so much in that "actions speak louder than words," (they often speak softly and subtly) but in that they do speak in response to each other, answering and rebuffing. Once we realize this, we'll see that we are rendering a *dialectic* of voiceless activities.

« »

The professional historian's phrase, "the dialog of events," is a good working metaphor. He does not thereby personify events;

he is not allegorizing. But he is storifying in earnest—giving character to eventuation. For skill in fiction is more than a contriving of events; it is a way of letting them "converse" with each other in a sequence that tells the reader what the author wishes to say with his story as whole.

He may also feel he simply has a good story to tell and that he doesn't mean anything special by it. That's an honest, modest attitude. A story can be *very* good in just that way. But as he comes to know his successive stories and his developing self better, he'll feel more and more that he's getting to know what he and his stories have to say.

This is what might be called an "occupational" phenomenon. The more we learn about how to write the less can we avoid saying something.

« »

It is not always the colorful oddities of diction that characterize people. Just as a person may have in his walk a characteristic rhythm, he has in his way of talking a rhythm that tells us much more about *him* than what he may be saying.

There is also the rhythm in the exchange of remarks between one speaker and another. It can give to your written dialog the convincing similitude you are after.

In the conversation you have been overhearing, the back-and-forth rhythm may not have been as prominent as you would be wise to make it when you write the dialog based on the colloquy. Be unafraid of stressing, or even exaggerating, the rhythmical; it is your surety.

« »

A person's *way* of saying something is also *what* he is saying. Both rhythm and the matter are always, in a story, his assertion of himself, and every such assertion is incremental in his characterization, regardless of how impersonal a tone he may affect.

This rhythm of his is also an aspect of the movement in the story at that moment. We can't expect the reader to take cognizance of this; nor should we. What we desire is that it should work on him.

« »

When we are overhearing conversation in another room, we'll be repaid for listening intently to the rhythm of it, especially if we are missing many of the words. If we already know the conversers, we can come near to making out what they're talking about. If we reproduce that rhythm in a dialog, we'll reinforce its meanings and dramatize its mood.

# Orientation

Narrating is like traveling. Only by bearing in mind where we are can we know in what direction we are going. At every move we have to be no less aware of the take-off point than we are of the get-to point. Narrative orientation is knowing just where we are in relation to all else in the story.

It is a consistency in using one or another point of view. This helps greatly in holding a story together.

Keeping ourselves constantly mindful of orientation transcends technique. It sustains our morale in facing complications and it supports our reader's desire to keep going on with us.

« »

In an intelligent response to a story it is as essential for a reader to know with every advance exactly who is doing the seeing, thinking, or feeling as it is for him to know who is speaking.

If we write a story without being clearly purposeful every time we shift from one point of view to another, we may as well do without quotation marks and he-saids in the dialog and not even bother to state where and when the dialog occurs.

« »

Some writers confess that they let themselves move around freely from one point of view to another, and they would feel inhibited if they didn't. This is true. You should not only let but also urge yourself to be conscious of everything that may be happening, of what this or that character might be any time feeling or thinking. But this is *your* freedom, not your story's.

It cannot be a skitter-scatter of consciousness and still have its full possible force.

The masterly control of point of view is primarily for your own assurance: that you're taking hold of everything and being boss. Your story, like your horse, prefers that.

« »

The more delicate the tissue of the story, the more vital to it is tension and the more disastrous any small rent in that tissue. Writers who believe themselves to be presenting matters too elusively impalpable, or too mystical, for a concern with the point of view are only concealing the fact that they are too clumsy to sustain in the gossamer they have spun the tension needed to make a story.

« »

By knowing how to maintain a single point of view, for instance, you can give your story a powerful focus: a concentration that will intensify what you wish to present dramatically, that will subordinate what you wish to keep from getting in your way. It will give your narration a core, however complex the situations and the action.

By having a deft control of the *shift* of point of view (from the narrator to character and vice versa, from character to character, and from the outer—objective—aspects of a character to his inner—subjective—experience or thought and vice versa), you afford your narration mobility and flexibility.

« »

There are successful writers, good and bad, who seem to be indifferent to the element of point of view, or they shift it erratically. Even though sometimes this capriciousness favors the caprice that the story itself intends to be, oftener than not the transilience gets out of hand, and the story rattles itself to pieces. To feel in control of the points of view affords you enough confidence to play with them freely without wrecking the story.

« »

Sometimes the subject, or the vivid detail, or the vivaciousness, or the violent action of a story impresses a reader so much that he himself cares no more about the mishmash of the points of view than did the author. These other elements were so powerful, or amusing, or brilliant, or zany that his attention was captured completely by them. Usually, however, a second reading of such a story is disappointing; it has a flimsiness or a bumpiness that the reader had at first overlooked.

« »

Shifting the point of view is shifting the interest. It cannot be otherwise, since it is shifting from one viewer to another. Each viewer is different, and so the interest of the viewing must be different.

« »

The time-honored way of viewing, still as good as ever, and the simplest, is that of the impersonal narrator, who is the unseen, unmentioned teller. He is the author with all his senses and sensitiveness and style but without his "I," so that to the reader absorbed in the story the I-less narrator is a non-person. The story then seems to be telling itself. Or the voice of the entire human race, or of the entire community or country, seems to be telling it. This voice has a kind of omniscience—a modest omniscience, for it is moderated to meet the moment-by-moment requirements of keeping the story going.

Now and then this omniscience acquaints the reader with this or that character's unspoken thoughts or feelings. But this is done as a quick, brief insight, and in a kind of *interpretative* manner, almost detached, so that there is no momentary chance of confusing the narrator with the character. The interest must not stay within the character's mind long enough for his personal view to seem to prevail as the basic or the central point of view of the story. And these inner moments should not be many, either. The prevailing interest of the story should continue to be objective: we see the characters and their scene objectively. Even when we have a peek into their hearts, that peek is offered not as a subjective experience but only in passing and only for our objective enjoyment. This plain dealing, this largely external recounting, has a nobility in it whether the story has the small dimensions of an ingenuous fairy tale or the grand dimensions of a novel.

« »

Although the old "omniscient" point of view continues to be plausible if its in-and-out (subjective-objective) management is discreet, a more easily plausible all-around point of view is one that is not omniscient but at least ubiquitous. That is, it's everywhere except inside any of the characters. It might be called the viewpoint of the eavesdropping ghost. It sees everywhere and hears everything. But only sees and only hears. If any inner feelings or meditations are narrated, they are spoken either by the character who has them or by another character who is intuiting about them out loud as he converses with or about the first character.

This can be enjoyable to write, because it beats the stage and screen at something like their own ploy. You can let and watch your characters do their own thing, almost as if for you only, none of them knowing their destiny nor that you do.

« »

A story can deal with many locations but it must itself be only one, either a single point or an overall position. To make a story by combining the two is nearly always like combining two different photographs by putting one of them upon the other.

« »

The subjective point of view is entirely centered within an individual. Interiority is the operative site, the psychological locus, of the story.

It will serve for an entire novel or for one or another chapter or "part" or "book." That is, the formal divisions accommodate the shifts, if any, from one point of view to another.

« »

The writers who do not know what they are doing when they intermix the subjective and the objective—so that they have no point of view, or point *for* a view, and in the final showdown really neither point nor view—are often too self-involved to be competent artists. They mistake their introversive habit or malady for introspective prowess, when they are writing about themselves; and when they delude themselves that they are writing about others, they mistake their self-indulgence for insight.

This compulsive introspectiveness plays havoc with the point of view; and since sensitively talented people are likely to be thus afflicted, this very defect is often fallaciously esteemed as artistry.

« »

The haphazard mixing of the subjective and objective aspects of a character leads into the absurdity of seeming to be inside his mind, immersed in the deep broth of his most private feelings, and at the same moment seeing his face and motions as other persons see them and as he never possibly can see his own exterior.

Oddly, this absurdity can have a point if indeed the writer has any idea he is making that point. It is a case of hitting upon a subject that calls for double aspecting.

For example, in stories about adolescent girls getting themselves in and out of alternately silly and serious difficulties, this subjective-objective placing of the point of view expresses frivolousness by matching it. Interior and exterior details may be noted in such rapid and mixed succession as to seem simultaneous, and thus in a quasi-unity.

« »

With writers who know what they're doing (particularly writers of animal fantasies, in which animals are dressed like human beings and thus are parodies of them), the simultaneous subjective–objective aspecting lends us the equivalent of the gift to see ourselves as others see us, inside-out and outside-in. For satire that is both shrewd and charitable, this is a superb device; it is delicately manipulatable. It is to be used on fools and therefore never by fools, except those of us who know our follies by knowing our skills.

« »

If we wish to focus the entire story within the character so that it it is *all* subjective, we will naturally tell the whole account in his language, using his vocabulary only, both in his uttered speech and in the narration. In that case, the only objectification you can hope for will be that which will take place in the reader's mind. He emerges from immersement in the character's world and returns to the world outside the character, and this external world then becomes emphasized by the contrast with the oddness, the individual spell, of the character's inner realm. But this monodramatic presentation of a story, with its advantages and disadvantages, is not at all the same as that in which the author narrates objectively while he reveals the inner world of a central character.

« »

Despite the quarreling between the champions of the poetic mind and those of the scientific, there are fiction writers whose art is a containment of these conflicting modes of observation, the subjective and the objective. These writers themselves, in temperament and education, combine an extraordinarily sensitive imagination with a disciplined rationality. They have read literature feelingly for its utmost subtleties and they have learned mathematics and one or two other of the strict sciences well enough to be respectably conversant in them. So, in their characterizations, their empathy is gentle and sure. They can produce the exact mood, the trance, of being within a certain person's self-consciousness, and yet do so from a position of detachment, so that they and their readers continue to be well aware of the world outside of the character.

The technical factors in the management of the point of view are fairly simple.

First, we limit for the entire story the subjective point of view to a single character. It is only into *his* mind and feelings we enter and *report* what is felt and thought there, and into nobody else's at any time. If the inner thoughts or feelings of any other character are necessary for the story they must be expressed by that character, or guessed by another character, in the *dialog*, and never in our report. The only inner experience, the only subjectivity, that we report directly, is that of our central character.

And, secondly, we make that report in *our* language—in our words, making full use of our verbal powers and allusive resources. The only time when any of the presentation is in the central character's words and thought-rhythms is when he is speaking, either out loud to somebody else or silently to himself. But then we have it clear that it is he, and not we, doing the talking at that particular moment.

It is here where the failures usually occur in the story combining a character's subjective point of view and the author's objective observations: the writer makes the mistake of presenting so much of the narrative in the character's language that the offward observation position is lost.

« »

The fictional feat of using the subjective point of view of a single character while retaining the detached position of a penetratingly perceptive narrator is not a mixing of points of view; it is not an attempt at the impossibility of being in two places at the same time; it is not a palimpsesting of one observer's (author's) account over another observer's (character's) account, like a double-exposure photograph. It is rather a combination of sensitiveness and control.

The intensity of the imagination probing into the experience of a character can be so great as to seem unbearable, and there are readers and writers who shrink from it (usually the kind who seek to be compassionate but who are only sentimental); but the author, and his reader along with him, project this deep empathy from the good distance of their generally shared realizations in the external world—external to them as well as to the character. Thus, instead of a double expressionism we have a double realism: we experience what it is really like to be that character with his delusions, prejudices, hallucinations, and so forth (that is, we see the reality of the existence of that individual experience) and yet we do this from the position of what is for us the abiding reality of our general experience. We enable ourselves to know a subjective drama objectively.

The distance we take is both aesthetic and scientific, for we not only know but we also know our way of knowing. If we do all this without here and there putting in our homiletic two-cents worth we are using personal impressionism as a means and impersonal naturalism as a method. Thus, it is probably in fiction alone of all the arts, that such a validation is possible. The work is risky, bringing the writer one grief after another, but worth it.

# Depth

A good writer may be wise in not trying to seem deep. This is akin to the civility of refraining from grave sententiousness in conversation. Like an honest way of looking honest, openness can be appealing; it can be an advantage to a writer who has a good deal to say that is not easy to say and so must be generous rather than awesome.

This candor does not preclude wonderments. A writer who keeps his imagination active throughout his work expects to waken his reader's imagination again and again.

Nor does an ingenuous openness have to be shallowness. Your writing is not inevitably superficial when it has a way of letting in plenty of light so that the details are sharp and their relationships clear. You may have a way of conducting the mind so gradually into profundity that for a good while there is no sensation of depth.

« »

In the art of writing nothing is more susceptible to fakery than depth. Let us consider two ways in which a writer may pretend there is depth in what he is saying.

One is the toilsome, explicit, complicated way. This is usual in poems elaborated to epical proportions, and in voluminous novels. Faked depths may seem impressive only because the reading has been made difficult. Ponderous words for lightweight meanings, unnecessarily complicated sentence structures for simple ideas, intricate approaches to petty significances, fancy mannerisms for plain matters.

The other way of simulating depth is that of being needlessly or shammingly implicative. Often there's a phony portentousness in it. It is likely to occur in stunted lyrics, heavily baked elegies, stories forced to seem somehow symbolical of who knows what, and other solemn shenanigans. Much as boys and girls will take on adult airs, some writers waste time and genuine talent in taking on an air of grave portents. Some ferret out of other writings the phrasings and intonations that seem to attend profound considerations. It is often only a gambit for a play that the secretly diffident writer knows nothing about. Or it's a naïvely shrewd bluffing of the reader who is expected to fall for it because of being loth to realize his own ignorance. If you have but little to say and you only half-say that, you can impress many a poor fool with thin hints of a deepness that isn't there. An understatement of a trifle can sound deeper than an on-the-level statement of something serious. There is no use or art in "leaving to the imagination" what you, the author, have not yourself imagined and what is not really imaginative.

« »

Illusion is invaluable in all the arts. Illusion of depth can be thoroughly honorable. In representational painting, this can be merely spatial and gratifying. In abstract or non-objective painting, illusions of unnameable depths are possible and these may occur in complexes that generate further depths. Either you see these depth illusions or you do not; if you do, there is no fakery; they are there just as actually as the canvas on the wall is there. In music, there is the "literal" depth of sound, which is made more interesting by the timbre of the voice or the instrument. There is also an emotional depth, which may be mostly the creation of the hearer and for which, as a whole, neither the composer nor the performer claims any credit. But there is sometimes in music an illusion of depth that is meditative in its character. The composer and the performer earnestly intend it to be there. It is an illusion and not just the stark structural design, but is a genuine experience. As we listen, the illusion of depth is unmistakable: as the music draws our attention closer it carries our contemplation of the sounds into what seems to be a deepening progression. (Music has also its depths that are neither "literal" nor illusive. They are conceptual and require a deliberative attention. We "listen into" firm structures of sound all the while we are following their development toward a formal completion.)

There are good writers who work well in depth but who have no interest in painting or in music. Among readers, however, those who have these interests are the more likely to be ready for the depths they come to in poetry and fiction. You have at least these readers to count upon.

The writer's difficulties with the illusion of depth are often greater than those of the painter or the musician. Painting or music might be called a language but neither of them needs *words*. Nothing else that is used in any of the arts has the uniqueness of words as an art medium: their might and their precariousness. The wordness of words is the writer's headache; and yet his main chance of doing what other artists cannot do is there, in the peculiar nature of words.

« »

There is a way to depth that is not sham: going way down into a subject, working deep into a character, having a character feel deep into an experience. There is no faking this depth; there are only ways of fumbling it. In the toilsomely elaborative attempt—

the painfully sustained pretense—there is no depth, only tortuous aisles and crazed coves of rubble. It is a failure even as a fake. But when you work in true depth, you have to watch where you are going, keep every change of direction in mind, make every move additionally significant, keep every preceding move as a propulsion to the further significances. This kind of work is structural as it "goes down" and is no job for a slouch. It *moves* deeper.

In narration, the motion of incident and the movement of events are a help to the writing and the reading; but where there is no narration, as say in an elegiac poem, these accommodations are absent. Some other process within the presentation (such as rhythm, *development* of symbol, *evolvement* of a conception, a formal device expressing change or progression in a pattern, and many another "activity") provides movement as an aid for following the deepening of the main thought.

# Criticism

## I

Let us dismiss from our considerations here the matter of spiteful criticism, which is like spitting on a red-hot stove and should spatter back into the spitter's face.

There's nothing else for us to do about it than to hate it, hate it so thoroughly that we always keep our stove red-hot.

« »

Literary criticism, more than any other kind, must be given and taken in good faith. This is because its medium, language, is also the medium of the object of criticism, and so what is baleful in the criticism becomes bad for the art. In no other form of literary expression is there more need for good faith between the author and readers. It's a kind of gold standard that becomes worthless with the least alloyage.

« »

Once a writer has exposed his work to public use, he is irrevocably set out for judgment. Then, only he can make the necessary transmutation of this into appropriate energy for subsequent work. Even the unfavorable or inane judgments. They come out of the same humanity that he is a part of. They are voices in the same world in which he lives. They belong in with his materials, at least. A good writer has no garbage problem; everything that comes his way is for recycling.

« »

The reason we are angered by helpful criticism which detects our faults is that we hate the possibility of being at fault. We are hurt by the realization. We loathe the bearer of bad news. The anger is the more roiling in that we subconsciously suspect all the while it is ourselves and not our critic who is to blame.

But the time comes when we hate the fault alone.

This happens over and over again. Do not expect that you will someday no longer feel anger over such criticism. You will always feel it. Let it come, let it go.

« »

Sensitiveness to criticism is a woe to the best of writers. And also an aid. The first thing to do is to note carefully just where it hurts. That examination is what leads to the wisest decision of the many possible decisions as to what next to feel, think, do. Any decision, though, must be based on the acknowledgment that there is no experience, whether painful or pleasant, that a writer can afford to ignore, and also on the determination that he will not be harmed.

Let it hurt, but don't let it injure.

« »

Your haters may be less vitiating to you than some of your admirers. A champion owes his prowess to his foes; to his friends he owes the sweetness of his slumbers.

« »

After each criticism however sympathetically given and good naturedly received, a healing cleanup is necessary, and nobody but you can do it for you. But do it. Do it at once, in whatever way you can: take a drink, say your beads, romp with your dog, climb an airy hill, fly a kite—anything actual and active and self-thanking.

« »

One should expect particular criticisms to be just as stimulative as they are corrective. Unfavorable criticism is a favor if it releases you from a cramp.

« »

Expect fine criticism to expedite you but not to outfit you. The instruments of a critical apparatus may be practical in the critic's hands, but they can get in the way of a productive writer who keeps many of them around. He has his own kind of tools and utensils, some of them made out of whatever he could lay his hands on during an emergency.

« »

Never tolerate a criticism or carry out a correction that would reduce the generative force of the poem or story you have written, lest that comment do so again with whatever you may write later. Your teacher, tutor, trainer, coach, or bosom-friend adviser cannot know this menace specifically; only you can. Never mistrust your own misgiving about any tendered advice.

Instead, trust your bewilderment. Look into it without opposing it, as a native venturing into a strange part of his home jungle, seeing with every step he takes the reverse aspect the scene will have for him on his way back. Or else feel the adverse tendencies in yourself as you wade through an opposing surf that will carry you back to safe footing.

« »

The writer should be able to read criticism as though he were writing it. His provisional identification of himself with other writers, inferior and superior to him, is a phase of the critical process—one which might be called "protocriticism" and one in which his adeptness affords him the opportunity of being a critic of critics.

A writer who does not often enough imagine himself writing the criticism he reads may neglect some skill in his own kind of writing or lose some cues for improvement.

« »

Very little literary criticism, whether written in early times or recently, is of practical help to the talented beginner, because so much of it is produced by the users of literature for the users, rather than for the future makers.

Writing is for most readers very much like a spectator sport. A cub baseball-player cannot learn from the opinions of sports reporters much about the rudiments or the fine points on how to pitch, catch, bat, work the bases, or field. Even the reporter who himself was once a player. A reader can only learn how to watch the game.

The practical advice a developing writer can derive from current reviewing is how to qualify for a movement in fashion at the time. And that can be the worst for him individually. By the time he will have mastered the tenets, the fashion may have passed.

« »

Many literary critics have an understanding of good writing only, the masterpieces. Too many believe the great works are the only ones worth bothering about. A growing writer gets little help from such critics. They have no understanding of bad or of crude writing. They are end-product handlers, and that is all. They know Literature, not writing. But because they presume that the analytical literary process exactly matches the integral writing process, they are forever unwriting what has been written. They are always progressing in a direction the reverse of the growing writer, proceeding from his goal back to his outset, conducting recursions of what were for him excursions, often uncharted.

« »

We watch writers who are alert to the critical emphases of the time, and we may become wistful about not keeping up with the leading critics; reading what they at the moment are reading. All this rue is wasteful unless we happen to have it within us *to produce* the compatible thing. If we have, we can thank criticism for having cued us. If we haven't it *to produce*, we must content ourselves with staying close to our own job, regardless of critical vogues.

It's better for us to think of critics someday feeding on us than to keep ourselves anxiously on the *qui vive* for every opportunity to feed on them.

« »

Bear in mind that whatever is observable is usable. Even the ways and wiles of critics. The world contains more materials for the poet and the fictioner than it does for the critic.

« »

A writer in trouble may receive excellent help from a critic who is in even worse trouble with his own writing.

A good critic may be a cruel one who knows your badness, which may be no worse than his own; he may be angry with you because he may know your potential goodness better than you do. (And maybe because it is better than his.)

« »

*Criticism*

An enlightening critic is more than a mental bundle of a vast amount of reading; he is a distillation of it. He makes a fine, steady light.

« »

It is an old snarl to say that unfavorable criticism is motivated by jealousy. The malady is not characteristic of all critics, nor of them only. It afflicts many other writers too, many who try hard to avoid sounding like a critic.

Oddly enough, it is the reader who is free from jealous feelings who is most likely, as well as most justly, to find the vocation of criticism attractive. (The chances are that among the finer critics, there are more with an *un*jealous temperament than there are among the finer poets and novelists.) This freedom from jealousy gives a critic (as it does any other kind of writer) an alacrity, an intellectual zest, that is soon evident.

More than that, with the critic it may be a special kind of freedom from jealousy, so special that it is what makes him a critic rather than any other kind of writer.

« »

It's a curious fact that when we are at an ebb in our production of poems or stories, many of us often find that we tend to skip those of other writers in a magazine, and go nosing into the critical articles instead. Why? Can it be because we feel that the same is being skipped within ourselves? Because we don't want to be alone with our ebb and so would make it universal? But there's also the converse curious fact: that when we're prolific we have zest for the kindred productions of others too. Creativeness then is attracted to creativeness.

It seems that when we're not producing, we dread as a kind of vicarious hard work (that is, we "write" as we read) a poetical or fictional production by anybody else. Critical matters seem then more interesting, and we enjoy the position of seeming to be an *amicus curiae*.

« »

If another writer is in your estimation 98 percent bad and only 2 percent good, you must reckon with that 2 percent. Not in justice to him, nor because you owe him at least that amount of fellowship. The reason is that you have to keep your eye in good training.

« »

To read poems and never have a thought of what your comment on them might be—to read poem after poem and have the writer's presence come to you through them, not once thinking of what you might say about him to others—*that* is the fundamental writer in you, The writer alone, without the critic.

In the midst of love we do not discuss love, nor do we analyze in the midst of poem and story. Afterward, yes. A writer must know the difference between an afterwarding activity and the many forwarding ones that occur from the start.

« »

It is futile to cry out against the existence of critics. We shall always have them with us. Each of us is in himself partly a critic.

Our minds are explicating, interpreting, categorizing, judging our experiences as though they were not *our* deeds or offside complicities. Our dreams and wakeful fantasies are incessantly reading between the lines of our private histories in order to predict evaluations.

Even the shadow each of us casts in sunlight, moonlight, lamplight, or spotlight is a kind of criticism, and becomes much more of a criticism if we try to trample it out.

Few artists can make a profession of criticism and continue to be artists. But as surely as you are an artist you are potentially a critic.

## II

There are plenty of criteria available for you by which you can judge much, if not all, of your work objectively, as your readers may, if you are willing to do so.

There are also such intuitive criteria as those you may glimpse in your private view of distant possibilities. They are there where you see them but you can scarcely name them. They may not need names since you don't expect to talk about them. Nor should you expect them to come on call. They may be harbingering hints of what's going to be uncommonly best to do. Or they may be precautionary hints of uncommon badnesses in the offing.

This inner criticism becomes more frequent as a writer matures and would seem to have a lessening need for it. But this need increases. That's because his temerity also increases.

« »

Some good poets are also good critics, largely because they were poets first. The reverse of this doesn't work so well. If there's any sure endangering of the poet by the critic, it happens within the same person.

Criticism, like the rudder of a ship, functions aft.

« »

Prophylactic don'ts tend toward a negatory cast of mind. We put anxiety into avoiding suspicions of guilt when we should be feeling eager for possible surprises. Some writers are too meticulous at first because they can't bear to be severely scrupulous afterward when they do their revising.

« »

The point to keep in mind when making revisions that are the consequence of good criticism, whether from others or yourself, is that the occasion should be to you, and *feel* to you, as a renewed opportunity. And one mostly for putting more, *still* more, imagination rather than the least bit less into the work at hand.

Revising should be essentially a re-envisioning. That is, seeing the work afresh—regaining the first fervor you had for it, which may have been spent during the vicissitudes of the initial composition. Unless that fervor was a mistaken one, or one that you did not see for what it really was, almost everything you may have to correct by revising, you should regard as accidental. Not as a deep defect in you or in your idea.

« »

Always seek return to at least your *inceptive* impulse if you have somehow lost the subsequent tenor of it. This doesn't always require rewriting, although just that may be what you feel most like doing. If so, there's nothing wrong and there's almost everything right about being born anew. Going back over and over can prove to be not toilsome but reviving.

And in all this, *expect* the corrections, mechanical or otherwise, to click into place eventually. As for polish, don't ever try for it. Let it too occur of itself in the main process, the very friction of that. Or not at all. It's the writers who are always striving mainly for finish who come to the grief of never getting started again.

« »

If the rewriting of your story generates more imagination in you than showed in the first draft, if the rethinking and revoicing of it precipitates more of its immanent substance, you can feel assured a similar phenomenon will occur in your true readers.

Really, that's what a good story should be expected to do. That's what distinguishes very good pastime fiction from the still better kind, which is incremental as time passes.

« »

When emendations occur to us after a regrettable bout of writing—ah, then we can have the blissful triumph of "getting back at" our adversary, the imp which is our fallible nature.

This is an out for the writer who shrinks from the self-rebuke implied by any need for making revisions. The dread of acknowledging one's wrong, particularly in any creative labor, soon becomes a superstitious feeling that the acknowledgment is what produces a wrong; and this silliness is typical oftenest of writers who like to keep themselves believing that they work only when they are inspired. A fallacy resulting from the notion that inspiration is infallible.

Divine as we may credit the source of an inspiration to be, we human receivers of it receive it humanly, and can do no other. Actually, our recognition of our faultiness and our pluck to take the risks are stimulants. Inspiration often becomes surprisingly active during the process of revision. Against his imp the writer has the last word.

« »

An actively imaginative writer may be adept at originating impressive theories about writing. Or some critical values. And other writers may take to one of them with aplomb and profit. But sometimes he can't. He can wonder about it, and yet try as he may he can't make it go with his peculiar nature.

On the other hand, he may have some other critical idea of his own that after further reflection he will dismiss as wrong, and then forget. But because of the pervasiveness within him of the creative, the idea may later sneak into the process of a new work of his, without any of his conscious notice, and prove to be a most righting and telling force.

« »

The critic within can browbeat the writer within. Can become *oppressively* authoritative. The writer in you must be wise to the fact that the critic in you can be misunderstanding, irrelevant, tactless, unfair. You have to put up with this seemingly internecine condition of selfhood. The experience of it sturdies you for being outspoken toward ever-querulous humankind.

« »

There's such a foolishness as straining too much to be sure of not saying anything trite. Once a writer gets himself into this fix, the very virtuosity he would summon tightens the cramp. The only specific that can loosen him from it is to go ahead and do some of the downright bad writing he's capable of. There never was a writer who did not have this perverse capability, though only a sagacious few will cheerfully acknowledge it. We cannot too often repeat to ourselves the wholesomely humiliating fact that unless we're willing to write badly when we must, we can't hope to write well as often as we'd like to.

The writers who cannot get used to this idea have the same frailty that all fatuous exhibitionists have: they can't bear not to be in public view most of the time, and as conspicuously as possible, whereas the true-to-himself artist uses just the reverse in this proportioning. Most of his time must be reserved for privacy. He needs this for his inevitable badnesses. And his still latent virtues. (These two are usually not adversaries within him but concomitants.)

« »

The chances are you won't unwittingly employ a cliché unless you once admired it a little, perhaps as a bit of glibness you wished you had thought of first.

As a fresh-minded writer, you develop a sensibility that quickly distinguishes between a new, often swank, cliché, and what might be called a proto-idiom. The difference, or the early sign of such, is in the element suggested above: between the spuriously individual and the genuinely common. For idiom has in it from its earliest utterance the desire for language, and the other the yen for style.

« »

The well-trained writer may estimate himself by his sense of the extraordinary and his way with it; the extraordinary writer, by his way with the ordinary and his instinct for its validities. Both minds quickly sense the difference between the obvious and the open or straightforward, the trite and the idiomatic, the stereotype and a utility.

Both minds, certainly, may be in the same person. When the critical and the creative are not afraid of each other, and not overworshipful, they get along together as united forces.

« »

He who feels the virtue of his clarity exults in it. For him there can never be too much. Clarity is not baldness nor rawness. It is light, plenty of light. There is nothing obvious about the full moon. Or its thinnest phase in a clear sky.

« »

If a writer feels compelled to strain against the familiar or to twist and kink his style against appearing too plain, he either doesn't know what it is he has to tell the world or he's afraid that only by being at odds with himself can he exhibit a way of writing that will be regarded as a departure from the humdrum. There's such a folly as the obvious avoidance of the obvious.

« »

Almost anything you force upon your work to fend off the criticism of obviousness only makes whatever may have to be said less said.

If a fact, be it ever so familiar, has to be cited or repeated for any of several reasons (it may have slipped the reader's mind at that moment, or it has a nuance of meaning as it clicks into a changed context, or the reader may not happen to think of it because of the dominance of the surrounding thought), then it must be given.

*Criticism*

You have to see supremely well the *nature* of the fact, which is its truth, to know what the supreme form of its utterance shall be.

« »

Many writers whose talents are striking have little depth of feeling and little penetration of thought. They proceed along safe, success-likely levels that have become hardened by constant trendings, or else they make audacious deviations that seem thrillingly excursive to their readers but that also are strictly according to the modish requirements.

If we consider their substance, the amount of inherent banality such writers manage to avoid is prodigious.

Their exact conformity to some vogue that is being specially used in order to appear extraordinary could hardly be matched even by the obedience of nuns in medieval times.

Fearing to be accused of obviousness, they strenuously maneuver away from the easily statable but needed fact as though the need were not there.

In that kind of elliptical writing to avoid the obvious such writers succeed only in evading their own power of forthrightness. They twist and dart and wiggle to avoid platitudes on their plane of thought, which nevertheless keeps on being just as flat as it is slick.

Their showmanship never attains to drama, inasmuch as drama is catastrophic in a way that strengthens the mind by imperiling it.

If you are a deep-going writer the chances you take of coming to disaster would make the surface writer shudder. But if you come through alive, the most striking feature of your production may be the simplicity of its means as compared with the complexity and power of its meaning.

# Momentum and standstill

## I

Laymen wonder how columnists, cartoonists, and other professionals in skillful expression can keep on turning it out year after year. "Oh, maybe he has ideas sent in to him that he pays for" is the usual answer. But the professional knows that the answer is in the *momentum* of his work.

With the writer, momentum is an achieved continuality of the imagination's motions within him. The achievement comes through using them, rarely if ever neglecting them, and sheltering them wisely.

« »

Writing must always be to the writer the *act* of writing, in whatever he might be thinking or doing, even at those times when he is not mindful of the fact and doesn't want to be. Even when he is idle, his momentum is not, and he knows it isn't. It's like a faith. A faith is never idle.

If you understand this you are virtually a writer whether at the moment you are fooling around in a boat up a mud creek or fooling around at your desk.

Between the activity at the desk and the action in the story there is a shared boon. Also the movement in the poem. Continuality. It keeps going on, like the circulation of your blood.

« »

When a writer's mind is intent upon a "goingness" in his story or poem, he almost forgets that the "goingness" of his personal industry is accompanying it.

It may be a most difficult story or poem to write, with many a frightening halt in the building operations, but this is not a cessation of the essential momentum, which is already there in the life of the characters and in their approaching fates, and is already in the motion of the poem thus far in its evolvement. Only if the writer has a static conception of his story or poem—only if he thinks of it primarily as something which exists solely that he may enjoy the gratifications of his having been its author—is any stoppage likely to be a deadly one. Otherwise the workings that were going on will tend to bring him back to producing it.

« »

In modern life, with an array of writing implements and surfaces available, a writer has many ways of keeping in motion.

He may make as many drafts as he feels necessary. He may enjoy pauses and tolerate delays in his production. He can put it aside for a while and come back to it, and most of this process is external to him.

He may condition himself so that when he is away from his desk, his receptive mind goes with him, but the ideas that meteorically flash into it, instead of burning up there, are somehow saved and gently lowered into his subconscious, whence they reappear the moment he is again at his desk.

Or his industrious habit of cogitation may go closely along with him on a vacation, like a wife who wishes to keep on doing the cooking away from home. He carries on his writing in his head while the rest of his mind and all of his body may be elsewhere employed, or blissfully idle. So what he will have before returning to his desk will be a mental draft of the work in progress. He has maintained a momentum during a vacation instead of during a workday, but the creative force is the same one. And it's the same as that which goes on during a toil-bent "thinking walk" when he carefully memorizes as he composes.

This kind of writing-momentum, let us not forget, is the oldest and most genuine. It was anciently what a writer *ordinarily* used, because writing surfaces were so scarce and implements so laborsome that *a* draft was usually the final one. To be sure, the writing-momentum as a thinking activity must have continued into the graphic phase, and this graphic phase did have its effect upon the expression (as it always does) so that "writing" became the true name for the entire creative phenomenon; and "style" in its metonymy of the stylus, became the entire man. But still the priority of the mental phase was dominant. One did so much of his writing in his mind beforehand (and before hand!) that we infidels today must realize he had respectable reasons for believing God was the author of certain surpassing poems, narratives, and announcements, and that the writer was simply one of the writing-tools in the process. This is how much force is possible in expressive momentum.

## II

It's good to feel your muse over your shoulder: "Go on, go on!" But her voice will fade out when you try hard to be brief. For then you're stinting your excursion in the very act of completing it.

« »

Imaginative writing is a generative act; it should also be generous. It must give forth. It is not a business of suppression. To begin by withholding will not control incontinence but may instead forbid expression. Once you get no-no-no in motion it will be as hard to control as yes-yes-yes.

If a writer is confident he has plenty to say, his ordinarily prevailing sense of relevance and continuity and rhythm helps by itself to govern his output.

« »

It is *usually* easier to trim excesses afterward than to make up a deficiency that was imposed at the start or within the process.

Accept the fact that creativeness is an extravagance. Reject the fallacy that the conflict between "letting go" and "holding back" produces a kind of aesthetic, or moral, "tension"; that there is here any valid analogy to the taut string of a harp.

But *often*, for many writers it is seemingly impossible to take a composition of theirs and reduce its mass without wreaking serious damage to its form or tone or to the flow of its reader-holding current. The severed continuity is no longer fluid.

When a composition has become too massy and yet too fragile for reduction or alteration, the only thing to be done is probably to accept its failure—to be content that even as an unfortunate performance it attained at least completion. And begin all over again. Write an entirely new version. Many a fine work has had such a history.

« »

When you have failed through overwriting an unalterable piece, try going back to your first spark of intimation that there was a poem or story ahead. Perhaps you lost the light of that priming spark.

Always go back to the freshness of your inception; it is your true and abiding innocence. You are likely to lose it again only if you insist upon scaring yourself with the bugbear of brevity.

« »

If there is too much long-winded writing in books it is not always because authors did not try to be brief. Many of them did try—at the wrong time. They tried at the outset, as the speaker does who opens an inevitably long discourse by saying he "will be brief."

« »

Write like a bird flying. He does not keep count of his wing strokes but keeps looking at what he wishes to get to. That is the shortest way.

## III

You can compress advantageously only what you have expressed adequately. Never pre-edit.

A tiny grain of extraordinarily fine dye spreads its color through water many millions of times greater in volume. That kind of "brevity," which when it occupies a sympathetic consciousness expands grandly, is not so much a compression as an intrinsic richness.

« »

"Compression" has become a cult of baking poetry into a hard-tack—in many instances to avoid the imputation of staleness where freshness is unlikely.

"Necessary compression" has become a haughty cliché to condone unnecessary obscurities. But compression is really necessary only when there is sparseness and looseness. In a poem or story with such a defect, once you have brought the few rich particles into a secure coherence you get form, not compression.

Forget about compression. Your primary reason for not bothering with it is not so much the difficulty you impose upon the reader by devising congested symbols, as the gnarling of your own mind. Do not be anxious about having world enough and time to say something; take a lover's space and tempo.

« »

We might well watch the calligrapher as he proceeds across the page with his pen. It is not a fickle instrument, but it will finick here and run away there. When it runs away, its mischief is not ugly, only wayward and a little thriftless. Ugliness occurs when the calligrapher hurries the pen to shorten his working time, or constrains it to move within too small a surface. If he does not heed his own best working tempo so as to keep it congenial with his pen's easiest pace, his hand will mangle certain forms that his eye understands capably.

All factors in action here (eye, hand, pen) "realize" that the form of any letter is shaped by rhythm as much as by preconceived design. No eagerness, no precious area, no requirement of compactness is worth the slightest sacrifice of that rhythm.

« »

In all arts rhythm demands prevalence. You can jazz a composition to surrealize it with rhythmlessness here and there, but this becomes expressive because it is really a withholding of rhythm rather than a destruction of it.

« »

Compressive brevity is a violence to rhythm. The rhythm of words might be there without the rhythm of the comprehending thought. You do not really enjoy a poem, either as its author or reader, if your thinking is hampered in keeping time with the wording.

« »

A richly radiant moment within a poem can be a miracle if it does not halt the poem or if the rest of the poem does not fall away from it like sloughed matter. Those momentary eternities cannot be isolates or compactions. They require the entire poem for their creation. Any moment in a rhythm is impossible without the whole rhythm. This concern is about the most favoring anticipation a writer can have for his poem.

## IV

Along with talent, knowledge, skill, and a subject the writer's vital possession is a momentum. Weak or strong, it is to be cherished lovingly.

Probably what more than any other thing makes the so-called "writer's block" is the misapplication of that dread phrase. The trouble may be nothing worse than natural fatigue. A restful pause should be enjoyed because it is good for your vigor. But that term "block" confers a kind of formal recognition like that given a de facto government, and the damn thing then can become too nearly real.

« »

Writers who have failed to get themselves started hope that some fortuity will give them an initial push; for all they know, they are late starters and nothing has been killed in them yet. But such a push is rare. And the hoped-for fortuity is almost always thought of as an external, whereas the real push is from within; and for those who have it, there is nothing initial about it. A propulsion seems to have started before you ever knew there was such a thing as authorship. You had been saying some intrinsically valued words to yourself, and remembering them and saying them over again; then when you learned the uses of a pencil you wrote them down. You weren't waiting to do this until you had time.

But if that wait ever begins, then a block has its chance to settle in. You become a yearner instead of a doer. The minimal momentum of a steady diarist or a vigorous letter-writer has the respect of the muses.

« »

A writer has to be ready to sacrifice a great lot to preserve his momentum. Usually, though, in a blockage the sacrifices that were evaded were not great ones, such as health or marriage, but petty ones. A hell of a lot of them. The thwarting factor in most cases is not a single, large importunity that you can note at once and somehow head off. Blindness and even paralysis have been shoved out of the way by a well-directed momentum. No, it's the cumulative, pesky little interferences.

Why, then, do we value them with any interest? It's because creative people must be indulgent in small ways toward all kinds of occurrences. But at the same time a hard shrewdness must develop.

« »

The saddest cases of blockage are those that result from misdirected ambitions. Usually the overweening kind. The idea of a great novel becomes the stymie to an excellent talent for rare sketches. The stopped dramatist subordinated in himself a brilliant epigrammatist. The would-be exquisite lyricist loses voice because he should have been writing the short story, which can receive its perfect tone from the lyrical wish. It's mistaken, not lost, identity that usually maroons the writer in a stuporous limbo.

« »

As our imagination dwindles we die. We die from the intellect inward and from the heart outward.

# Freshness

We who still dare to be poets and story makers this long after the early phases of our art face a difficulty probably greater than any that the first, crude venturers did.

It is not only that there is now in the general literate mind of the whole world an accumulation of achievements, which is like some dread monarchal catalog that prevails as a total and definitive claim of ownership. It is not only as though travelers had visited every part of the world and made every kind of observation of every witnessable feature and had worn thin every rhetorical means of telling about it. It is not only the vastly looming presumption that all that is humanly experienceable has been experienced and superbly recorded.

It is not only that everything that can possibly be felt and said about death has already had its best expression.

What then is it? It is that death has now a rival which intercepts it. Dullness. Pandemic dullness.

This is the greatest and worst bafflement that writers have ever come up against. Although they themselves are not dull, and although some of their hoped-for readers are not, either, dullness importunes itself upon both as an ineluctable subject. The insistent theme or endeavor is no longer one of finding a way for telling death not to be too proud, or for according it a kind of respect that redounds to our own dignity; the idea is to forestall or kick out dullness.

For a while the fashionable trick was to ornament it by using an affectation called ennui. It was like using perfume to disguise the need of a bath. Immature would-be sophisticates learned how to speak to anybody about anything in weary voices, implying a superior kind of boredom. And the hapless fools who tried to make something of it as a literary vein for attracting the plaudits of the smart set dwindled away.

Dullness is a pervasion into homes and mansions and churches and houses of state, even into the cellars of revolution. Each new generation with its novel defiances succumbs to dullness when not even the police (themselves perhaps victims of the same curse) can put them down.

Wherein is the relief, the restoration? In forages beyond the earth's gravity? In probings into its core? Where can we go, what think, so that dullness and the conquest of it will not be our chief subject?

Only one resort: our emotions. They are our only freshenings, our only reaccess to our spirit. We must relearn how to rage in anger, how to leap for joy, how to sing, to dance.

To begin a poem or story afresh, expose yourself to the emotion of it. Don't be afraid to *feel*. Dullness is the numbness that comes of being afraid.

« »

Once we have the courage to take back again our oldest feelings, even the ancient and the "pre-historic" ones, we need not worry about not having anything new to say or any new way of saying it. Death will not have changed but that immense complexity so oversimply named "life" will have changed. The two words *life* and *change* are virtually synonymous.

We are not in competition with the writers of the past. The changes in language since they had their say are due to changes in things, in landscape, in ideas and worship and ethics and us.

This is our big break. We're still as good as new.

« »

Theological thinking may be humbug to a writer but sooner or later his workaday thinking must accept the proposition that a writer, no less than any other man, must be born again. A writer's life is a series of rebirths, many of them agonies.

« »

Poets and novelists, after having devoted a lifetime to the cultivation of considerable talent, sometimes suspect themselves to be failures. This is a sorrow almost general in the profession. It is bearable only because the lifelong interest in poetry and fiction does not go sour; it has all along equaled the personal ambitions and now survives them.

« »

Like a man who has been imprisoned, then pronounced innocent and released, who now is so joyous in his restored dignity that he feels no bitterness, but in turn releases everybody from blame, we emerge from our dungeons of defeat and resume our vocation.

« »

To the modern viewer of literary history, the outstanding fact is the spread of publication. Because of this, information now covers more of the world than water does of the earth. This has affected writers so that sophistication seems to them to have become imperative. At least, there is a sanguine naïvety that to give the impression of sophisticatedness is to show that one is not falling behind, that one is alert to the newest.

Here occurs an irksome contradiction: though sophistication purports to be alive to what is fresh, and seeks to be disdainful of the stale, it is the sophisticated who would have you believe that experience destroys the "innocence of the eye," which if it means anything practical to a writer means freshness—not scathelessness.

To be experienced is to know much more and to know it better than one can who is only sophisticated; for the first requires our having lived through trying events with what feelings and thoughts we could bring to such trials, and the second requires little else than that we absorb experiences as we do information so as to be no longer ingenuous in our behavior: hardening our sensibilities in order to sharpen them, and by doing so lessen our sensitiveness.

A writer who wishes to come out of such a mess intact had better disabuse himself thoroughly of fallacious notions about the relation of experience to innocence.

« »

Not all of one's creative freshness is blithesome; most of it is shocking or tempering in a way that makes for unusual seriousness. The element of the tragic that has not changed with changes in the type of tragedy, through the ages, is the freshening of the seriousness in a myth or an idea. In tragic presentments, the renewal is much more than doing the same thing over again in a novel way; it is at least a change, if not always an increase, in ponderment.

« »

Biologists have found that, beginning with the most primitive cell, a hurt and survival after it is the way of organic life. Every living organism has evolved, and is continuing to evolve, because of its injuries; it otherwise could not have attained to any of its complexity (which for us is *interest*). We are the product of innumerable hurts, many of them grievous, some nearly disastrous. We are the sum of our scars.

In the creed of a writer this harsh biological fact can feel like an ordainment.

« »

Innocence, in its etymological sense of "unhurt" or "unmodified by any harmful occurrence," is an inappropriate term to denote the kind of fresh energy that a poet has at his best. For he can carry his fundamental "wound" through his growing up and maturing, and not lose this freshening power. This very capability of his it is that distinguishes the creative worker from the uncreative one.

Only when bitterness sets in and there is malice in your rebuke of life have you lost what should be meant by the term innocence of the eye or of the mind. Then no amount of the sparkle in the sterile wit of sophistication, no amount of desperate innovation against triteness, can suffice in lieu of the lost capability.

« »

Innocence in art is not artless, nor a lack of cleverness. It is guileless. It is not merely pure; that is not its prime value. It is sure. Its purity is that it is free from outside hindrance. Its sureness is its ready acceptance of its inner power.

« »

The innocence of the eye is an alacrity for looking at the world so that there is always a fresh activity in seeing. Experience can strengthen rather than weary this vision. Innocence in creativity is not an incapacity for maturing. An innocent talent constantly seeks exercise, and it can thrive in discipline.

« »

One can become so full of facts, that one becomes blind. One forgets what beauty facts can have.

Likewise experience can make one too expert. Over-practice can change second nature into mechanical motion. Critics and other writers who have aged instead of matured through sufferings and long observation of evil cannot believe an artist can mature through those same experiences and retain innocence of the eye. If those disbeliefs were right, there would never have been a tragic work. The one thing that gives a sorrowful account the dignifying aspect that we call tragic is the restored clarity of vision that is possible only in our essential innocence.

« »

No matter how much you may premeditate the deed, most of the vitality of what you will write will spring into being only while you are writing, and not before. Beforehand you might anticipate and clear away some of the difficulties, but the actual miracles that reduce fumbles to insignificance are most likely to occur during, and within, the actual process of the writing.

Many of the good things you program beforehand so as to feel secure you will perhaps lose forgetfully by the time you start. Then you will spend some of your most valuable writing-energy in an effort merely to remember them. And when you do recollect them the bloom of their spontaneity may be gone. A more or less definite plan ahead of the writing is mostly to the good—not so a great baggage of details. Even when none of these are lost in the transfer from their collection to their use, they may become stale or be impediments instead of live factors. Or, reluctant to give up some of the hardwon but irrelevant beauties, you may find yourself wasting your energies (*and plan!*) trying to contrive uses for them. (This is how a writer's note-taking will "show" like misfit underwear.)

Research, preparation, long sessions of theme-deepening contemplation are indispensable, to be sure. Do not let them, however, become obsessive. The newer thinking you will do as your fingers are carrying your thoughts onto paper can have the rarest freshness of any ideas occurring anywhere in the world at that moment.

« »

How can a poet so young be so wise! How can a poet so old be so fresh! How can music so solemn be so alleviating!

« »

What wisdom is to knowledge innocence is to experience.

« »

When we see a place for the first time, the impact of its real presence is likely to awaken our senses and our imagination in the same instant. The scene may be ever so old but our view of it is fresh. For that moment at least, we are in a state of innocence. If we have long inhabited a scene and then watch travelers arrive, we can see on their faces an inimitable innocence as the eyes get the first glimpse of that which we already know. And if our imagination is active we see that place having on it the same look it may have for those eyes. Our impulse for the restoration of this innocence has almost the same spontaneity as that which characterizes the innocence itself in its prime occurrence. We respond to the innocence of somebody else's response. This is what as writers we have to count upon. This "innocence of the eye" which seems losable is also catchable.

« »

To make out a dim star or to find the tiniest soaring bird, a side glance is quicker than a stare. We sometimes can see an object better after having closed our eyes to it. These are old tricks long known to marksmen, scouts, and pilots.

Another old trick is to quiet the mind, so that a restful darkness and weightlessness, a kind of void, is there for a brief while.

The "rest" is a willing suspension of a familiarity in order to enjoy an improvement of belief. The stale familiarity of what is so monotonously in plain sight as to elicit only indifference is an obscurity that lets us slump in a doze of chronic disbelief.

Look at a familiar landscape or person for a moment as though you were a stranger—by imagining the possibility of much in them that is as yet unknown to you. The reality of them will be freshened. Presence will overcome transience.

In the older sense of the word, it is we who *surprise* the object: we overtake it so as to get hold of it.

« »

We need to think often of the word "presence" as a verb, because "presencing" is what we try to do. This requires of us freshness of attitude and intent. To "presence" a character or action or scene or idea is much more than to present it. When we succeed, it's because of our own presence as a beholder of any of these, *our* freshness as a beholder. We make that freshness contagious. When a scene, or a flower, or a face loses presence for us, it is we who are not really there.

« »

Do not hesitate to be an imagist whenever you have a chance. The eye-and-mind that is keen at gemming for the expressive image with an adamant finality of shining beauty has a cunning which is always in style and which should be called angelic rather than devilish.

« »

In the long run a canny writer will prove himself a pragmatist. He has a two-handed mind. Innocence and experience, spontaneity and calculation, are freely contrapuntal on the literary instrument. We must not be afraid to play it.

« »

Wiseacres sigh ruefully, "Live and learn" after having made an expensive mistake. But the creative man reverses the maxim: "Learn and live." This is asking for more trouble. You have to unless you want the peace of death.

The story maker tries to find a way of making trouble more interesting. "They lived happily ever afterward" does not mean they died.

« »

Our inchoacies—we must never be ashamed of them. They will occur in our ripening phase and will not be entirely different from those we survived when we were callow. What of it?

This: a fresh idea is worth some moments of return to the awkward age.

Let's honor our inchoacies. Feel their destined dignity. Our work at its frailest deserves this respect of its closeness to what is spontaneous in us. Spontaneity in writing occurs only if we let our inceptions occur at the site of their origin.

« »

One cannot but feel that the poem or story one writes is somehow unique despite what shortcomings it may have. This feeling is not wholly conceited. It rises from the uniqueness of one's own conscious existence. This is the most fundamental assurance of any that anyone can possibly have.

Everyone's experience of life is unique with him, himself, despite how ordinary he may appear to others or how trite it may seem to him. Inasmuch as he may recognize the possibility of that uniqueness (even the uniqueness of his feeling his banality) and only if he does recognize it, there is within him the fore-yeasting of a poet.

« »

Many people cease learning how to use their eyes, especially their minds' eyes. Even the blinded cherish the eye of the mind, for this can continue as the eye of innocence. When this sight is gone, blindness is at its worst. Then even though we may have perfect optometric vision, objects no longer have presence, reality loses its realness, action its actuality.

If you endeavor to write for such people you can be sure of receiving a judicial reaction. It will be inconsequential whether laudatory or not. They live by classifications they have settled for, and they will stay within them like horses in a stable that is burning to the ground. You cannot budge them.

« »

Like a fine morning, when we think, "How morninglike the morning!" our cognitions should be surprising; they should "dawn" on us. Full of days as we may become, each morrow is as new a day as we are willing to be new to it. The day then is alive with our waking to it; we did not die last night. Full of guilt as was our sleep, the moment of waking can be an innocent one. In that moment may come the extreme throe, one so great that its magnitude is a newness, and our relation to it an innocence.

« »

Sophistication is having learned (mostly through reading) that April is cruel—and having been rudely surprised by the information. Wisdom is having expected the Aprils to prove crueler than the other months after all. Freshness, a poet's freshness, is the wisdom that expects forsythia to flash and lilacs to chorus, however harsh the winter was, yet feels surprise each time.

The innocence of poets is freshness of expectation, clarity of vision, response that is both quick and lingering, diminishment of guilt sickness through activity of gratefulness, readiness for further experience.

Innocence without experience is impossible. Even a seemingly passive infant is experiencing consciousness, and only after it has had some experience can it manifest its innocence.

« »

Innocence is not always bliss.

Blisses are rare, volatile. But innocence does not evaporate with them.

Innocence is often pain. Then pain has a purity of its own.

« »

We cannot repeat or extend a moment of innocence; every latest moment of it becomes earlier and earlier in our memory and yet we do not lose it, not if we tend our minds as we should. This is one of the reasons why many writers use their childhood for materials even though the thesis is maturity. Those early moments are like the pitch-notes of a tuning fork. But also, any important latest moment can be one in which there is for us a "childhood." If a writer cannot believe this he may as well be a blasé journalist, an expert for whom a sustained weariness is a boon, like a thick gauntlet that grasps, that lets one judge weights, but through which one does not feel.

« »

One's spontaneity is the first evidence of one's poetic vitality. A young writer may fear he must protect it.

If the protective device is "not talking" until after he has completed his poem or story, the caution makes sense, regardless of how much it may resemble a superstition. An actor can repeat a moment of spontaneity; this is largely what makes him an actor, rather than the author of the play, and an admirable virtue this is; but the writer must catch his first spontaneities as though they were sparks, each with its unique ignition for a certain kind of fire.

If the protectiveness, though, takes on its own prestige it may displace what it is used for. The device then becomes formal as a *manner* and dictates the performance of the composition. The manner, or mannerism, may be blatantly informal itself, but its employment becomes a formality—even a "style" for identifying the writer, as a trademark does a manufacturer—and that is the end of the beginnings.

There are writers who enslave themselves to their methods of liberation. Their very rhapsodism, in its perpetual clutter of spontaneities, becomes a deadening monotony. You cannot protect by multiplicity. If a natural species attempts to do so the result is suicide, and this happens sooner in any of our arts.

How then are you going to protect your spontaneity? The only answer is do not even try. Conduct it, instead. Do it the way a singer or a swimmer conducts breathing by going from one breath to the next with continuous profit, by knowing the sustaining rhythm that is your own and keeping *that* to yourself. This continuum does not become monotonous; each breath causes its successor, and the succession of causings is always freshening rather than fatiguing.

« »

To wonder is to redeem vulgarism. To wonder is to renew, to distinguish anew. Wondering is an imaginative way of knowing, for it combines our emotions and intellects. It is a moving-into and taking-unto way of knowing. It is the mind's springtime, and with it we again see things originate from the ground.

« »

To the poetic mind, wonder is in itself a kind of intelligibility. Such a mind does not frettingly berate another writer's verse or prose for being abstruse if it begets fresh wonderment. For one's poetic imagination perceives in a new wonderment what language cannot yet directly name. Language lags behind imagination.

« »

Wonder in the familiar is more prizeworthy than in the strange: the blossom-scent taste of an exceptionally fine ripe common plum, for example, as compared with the rawly novel taste of an exotic fruit.

« »

In our poetic intent we do not expect our reader to "wonder" what it is we mean, unless we too are "wondering" that. This, though, is only partial, uncompleted wonder*ment;* and there are times when we can do no better than to ask others to share our incompletions with us—but most justifiably when we feel there is probably universal community in that incompleteness.

Completed wonderment is what we intend most of the time, however, and this is neither stating some dismaying question or questioning some overpositive statement, but is beholding some verity in the awesome environment of its origin. Then we wish our reader not to wonder what we mean, but to mean the same wonderment as ours during an extraordinary contemplation. Then there is no occasion for tedious analysis and bickering explication. The wonder is simply there. Each of us—author, on to reader—enters it as casually as he draws in his own breath from the air that is everyone's.

« »

*Freshness*

Wonderment is the antidote to indifference. It is what we feel when we consciously participate in what the cosmos is doing. Just what that is we do not know but we know we are trying to find some way of knowing how to know it. This is giving us all we can do awhile. We are as capable of wonderment as we are interested. The dull, the stale, the grubbingly pious are not interested in what is wondrously real.

« »

"What is the meaning of it all?" writers, both the poetic and the would-be poetic, keep asking about the cosmos when their imaginations are doing only busywork.

Quit nagging at existence. So far as you can know, you are in essence as exactly its meaning as you can ever find out. Its meaning is not the question. The question is, "What is the experiencing of it?"

« »

Strike a weathered rock. The fracture reveals the true composition and content: glistening crystals, fresh color, story-telling grain, and so forth.

« »

Seek freshness wherever you can find it. Do not be afraid of innovation; do not scorn novelty. But discriminate. The better the genuine is for you, the more is the danger of the spurious. Understand change. It is the theme of life, and this means more in poem or story than "the meaning of life" can ever mean. It is *the* dynamic of the art of writing.

« »

All stories are metamorphoses.

A very good story may well be a chain-reaction of changes from the incipient situation to the conclusive one. And that finale then is, in contrast with those changes, an ironic stasis. For irony is itself a metamorphosis. And the stasis may be a significantly experienceable change from change to nonchange. Usually depressing. That is, death. Or else, marvelously serenifying. Eternity, perhaps.

What the fictioner must concentrate upon in these matters is the nature of change itself. The poet, no less so. Every trope is a metamorphosis. Every story is a trope. The poetic: the fictive. The instancing: the narrating. These are mutuals.

« »

It is just as unfair to impugn novelty for being short-lived as to scorn a tradition for being "too old." A toothless elephant starving to death is too old, and an airborne bubble collapsing is too impermanent, but both are fulfilments of their nature.

The nature of novelty is to be evanescent and of tradition to be durable, and in both instances our business is to make the best of those very natures. Then we can quit quarreling with our materials.

« »

A story does not move forward by rejecting its past. Even its very opening assumes a past. The past in time or story is formed by a passing onward. This is true even of so seemingly frozen a motion as a sculpture; the eye and hand pass around it in the same way as the mind does through a narrative. A past is denoted that continues effectual in the progress of our attention; it does not just stop. The true classic permanence is a sustained continuation.

« »

The reason an "immortal" work does not die is that it does not let us die.

« »

You can't achieve freshness merely through rebellion.

Blatant, self-styled "rebels" who go about yelling "away with" this and that are not clearing the area for fresh growth but for nothing. From nothingness there is no possibility of starting afresh. Freshness is always a somethingness.

« »

Make changes but make them incremental. Not all change is growth but all growth is change. So think of growth when you are seeking change, or freshness.

« »

A writer can be a stuffed shirt no matter now loud the colors and rampageous the pattern. But also he can remind himself that a rediscovery of classics can produce a renaissance.

Some innovations are so long in the making that they have had to begin in ancient times. A vehement nihilism in a writer usually becomes a stale stubbornness in less time than it takes him to wear out a pair of new shoes.

« »

Shock may accompany innovation but cannot produce it. Its best use is in upsetting complacency. It's a tactic, not a strategy, in wakeup writing. Least of all is it a *way* of writing. A writer must keep himself warned that when repudiation does not have creation follow it, it continues to repudiate without doing anything else.

« »

Free your mind of the question whether you are by temperament suited to the classic ways or to the romantic ways. Just don't waste your mental energies being against either. Living and writing today you are suited to both.

Both inhere in the same person although either may be so prominent as to seem to deny the presence of the other. One may have been unduly silenced because the other has been wakened, with special jubilance. Both may be awake and in conflict, or somehow reciprocally productive despite their opposition. Nowadays it is less than ever likely that a working artist can be gifted entirely for the one and not at all for the other.

He may have the highest respect for the Classical and aspire to perpetuate its dictates through good works, and yet find himself ever and again to be effectual in the Romantic vein only. Or it may be the other way around.

This perversity should not be defeating; we have tropes and metamorphoses in our art because they occur in our living. Each of us must face himself on this score and do so with good humor.

If a traveler keeps going northward he will find himself going southward, and he must accept the fact as of *his doing*, not the earth's.

We are writing *now*, in our nowness; we are interpreting what *is*, what is with *us;* we are not reading, historifying, re-searching into what was. We cannot find a refuge in some otherwhile and still have available to us our complement of inner power. And we must have that complement to keep ourselves freshened for each writing task. Even if that task is one of voicing an extremely ancient matter that must be given in the full spell of its ancientness. The less we worry about whether we are doing any of our writing in the classic or in the romantic vein, the freer we'll be to give it a freshness it could not have from anyone else.